Personal Development and Team Management

David James

FINANCIAL
WORLD
Publishing

Financial World Publishing
4–9 Burgate Lane
Canterbury
Kent
CT1 2XJ

T   01227 818687
F   01227 479641
E   editorial@ifslearning.com

Financial World Publishing publications are published by The Chartered Institute of Bankers, a non-profit making registered educational charity.

The Chartered Institute of Bankers believes that the sources of information upon which the book is based are reliable and has made every effort to ensure the complete accuracy of the text. However, neither CIB, the author nor any contributor can accept any legal responsibility whatsoever for consequences that may arise from errors or omissions or any opinion or advice given.

Typeset by the Alden Group, Oxford.
Printed by Antony Rowe Ltd., Chippenham

ISBN 0-85297-665-8

Contents

Contents

Contents

Introduction

In this book my main objective is to give you, as CCP students, a flavour of some of the key elements in team and personal development. The structure of the book follows sequentially that of the syllabus and looks to introduce you to various aspects of management. You will realize very quickly that many of the areas we look at are worthy of one volume, or sometimes several volumes, in themselves because there are many quite complex areas that you need to become familiar with, and have an understanding of as your studies progress.

What you will need to consider, throughout your reading of this book, is how you can not only learn and understand its contents, but also, crucially, how you can apply your learning in the workplace. Nobody has a finite level of knowledge of anything – it therefore follows that all of us, me included, can continually learn throughout our working lives. This book gives you perhaps the first opportunity to relate every section to your own organization and day-to-day activities. You will then begin to think about how theory relates to reality, what works well, what is not quite what you thought it would be, and also to consider trying doing some things in a different way.

I have thoroughly enjoyed writing this book, undertaking the research and thinking about its contents from your perspective. It is also entirely appropriate that I thank those close to me for their unwavering support while I have been busy being a course author. I am ever grateful to my wife, Elsa, and son, Oliver, for their incredible loyalty and support throughout. Also, grateful thanks again to my Mum and Dad who have been with me in every respect, and as part of this supporting my undiminished personal thirst for continuing to learn and help others to learn over a period of over 20 years. Thank you.

Unit 1

Planning

The Whole Process

During the pages that follow we shall be looking at planning and control primarily, but as I am sure you know, these activities do not and cannot happen in isolation; they are part of a much bigger picture and set of activities which can be charted as follows:

(1) *Defining (clear) objectives.*

(2) *Creating a plan of how to proceed.*

(3) *Making sure that each member of the team understands his or her role and responsibilities.*

(4) *Setting (possibly after debate and discussion) and agreeing performance standards.*

(5) *Creating systems to ensure that appropriate management information will be available to enable you as team leader or manager to track progress.*

(6) *On an ongoing basis comparing results against the performance standards and business objectives identified in points (4) and (1) above.*

(7) *On an ongoing basis throughout the plan, taking any remedial or corrective action if there are any differences between the plan and actual activities. If necessary, plans could be amended.*

1.1
Creating a Plan

One of the foundations of making good progress within any team or business unit is by planning what it is you are looking to do. The plan itself will give a structure of what is looking to be done, and will give you and your team something formal to measure progress against. Clearly, any plan that is produced needs to be relevant and realistic when compared to what can be achieved in reality. You will know what constraints are in place, for example, in terms of cost, timescales, number of people actually available to help to bring this plan to life, and so on. Nevertheless a plan must involve all resources that are available and relevant to the plan itself; this will include team members, machinery, budget and anything else that may be needed. Furthermore, particularly with regard to members of the team, you will need to consider what they can achieve in reality – both in terms of their current skill levels, and skill levels they may be able to develop either before the plan starts or during the life of the plan itself.

The plan itself will have many features and will look to:

- *Define concisely what needs to be done.*
- *Identify who is the 'sponsor' of the plan (for example, the team leader's line manager).*
- *Define the roles and responsibilities of each individual team member.*
- *Explain clearly how the various activities will be undertaken.*
- *Give clear indications of when the plan is to start, and the anticipated completion date. For some plans there will be 'milestones' in between and these may well be official review dates.*
- *Probably identify the likely location or locations where the activities within the plan are to be carried out.*

If a plan involves a team then, as we have seen in the list of features above, all (or most) of the team members will be involved. It therefore follows that an effective communication system must be in place so that all of the team, individually and collectively, are fully aware of what is going on. The whole team need to understand what the objectives of the plan are, and to have a specific understanding of their own roles and the responsibilities that each will have in making the plan a success. Ideally, the team leader will be aware of how each team member can contribute to the plan and be aware of each of their team member's strengths and developmental areas. Furthermore the team leader will need to be very clear about how each of the team members will be feeling throughout the plan and to provide support and guidance where necessary. The communication process will, in any case, need to be one that is 'two-way' so that on an ongoing basis not only are you as team leader conveying information about the plan to the team, but they are also able to come to you whenever they need to seek guidance and clarity, for example.

We have seen above how any plan should have specific performance standards within it. These standards will enable each team member to be clear about what level of performance they need to achieve. The mnemonic that you will often see to help to define a performance standard or objective (of a plan) is 'SMART', which can be expanded to mean:

- **Specific**

This means that the standards within the plan must be specifically stated in terms of what the team collectively and each individual within the team needs to do.

- **Measureable**

Each standard or objective within the plan should be capable of measurement. Examples of such measurements could include quantity, time, cost or quality.

- **Acceptable**

In reality some standards (or targets!) are often 'imposed' from higher levels within the organization. Ideally, however, any standards or objectives should be agreed after a mature and sensible debate between the team leader or manager and the team themselves.

- **Realistic**

Any standards, hopefully agreed after discussion between the team leader and the team, must also be realistic. There is no point whatsoever in having standards or objectives that are unattainable. There needs to be a balance between having standards that are challenging, and that can be achieved when all goes well, and the maximum use of all the resources available. Standards or objectives that are set too high will most likely have a demotivational affect on the team when those standards are soon seen to be way out of reach.

- **Time**

Within the plan, there needs to be a clear idea of how long the plan itself, and any parts within it, are likely to take. For example, a plan should have a start date, and a completion date. Regular progress checks will probably be included at regular intervals throughout the life of the plan.

1.2
Measuring Progress

So far we have seen that a plan has various constituent parts, and that communication is a crucial activity throughout the plan, and that having 'SMART' performance standards can be vital.

Again throughout the plan the team leader, and each of the team members, will want to know how they are performing against these performance standards or objectives. The way in which this can be done is to collect meaningful management information to enable an accurate assessment to be made of ongoing progress. When this management information is available, it will be useful only if the previous steps we have already outlined, namely the objectives of the plan are very clear (and known, understood and accepted by each team member) and the performance standards and objectives are 'SMART'. As a result, if accurate management information is available, the comparison between what is expected and what is actually being achieved should be reasonably straightforward.

Depending on the specifics of the plan being undertaken, regular review dates of progress against standards should be put in place; examples of such frequencies are monthly, weekly, and even daily. A balance has to be achieved between the actual cost and time that is required to 'monitor progress' compared to the actual improvements in the planned activity that may be achieved as a result. If performance against standards/objectives is checked too frequently, it may be cost ineffective. Alternatively, if these checks are too infrequent, then early warning signs may be missed, and by the time an official check is made, it may be too late for remedial action.

Once any deviations are identified, the next decision to be taken is what to do about them. There may be three possibilities:

- *Take any corrective action.*
- *Consider, amend and repair.*
- *Do nothing.*

In the first case there may be several causes for any performance deviations; examples include:

- *Poor working practices.*
- *Faulty equipment.*
- *Higher than expected staff turnover.*
- *Overexpenditure.*
- *Shortage of supplies of essential material.*

I am sure that you can include your own examples here to add to those given above. For some of these, there may well be ways in which performance can be placed back 'on track'.

In some circumstances, however, it may be that any deviation from the expected level of activity is looked upon in a different way – one possibility could be to conclude that the objectives of the plan were, with the benefit of hindsight, unrealistic. Possibly, the performance standards that were expected of your team members were agreed or set far too high. In these types of scenarios, it would be more important to review the plan itself rather than the deviations between ongoing activity and expected levels of performance.

The third option is to do nothing, which means that when taking into consideration the available management information, a (hopefully fully) informed decision will be taken that work can carry on in the knowledge that the overall objectives of the plan will still be achieved on time.

In any case throughout the whole planning process effective monitoring will be needed to make sure that the end objectives in their original format or amended during the course of the plan are ultimately achieved.

1.3
What Planning Is

Planning then is basically one way of looking to the future and working out how to achieve a series of objectives in that unknown future. We have seen that there is a clear need to predict the future as far as we can and to see what impediments are likely to be faced while trying to achieve a plan. Clearly, the element of projecting into the future cannot be done with total certainty, which means that any good plan needs to be adaptable to perhaps cope with any change that was not foreseen.

Any organization or business unit will not have only one plan to ensure that it meets it business objectives successfully. It will have many plans which cover various timespans. There may be, for example, short-term plans, medium-term or longer-term plans to cope with the various objectives a business may have. The longer the term the plan has, the more likely it will need to be adaptable to cope with change.

Here are some examples of different types of plans:

- **Strategic plan**
This type of plan would tend to be longer-term and look at the overall achievement of a business's objectives. Objectives within this type of plan will tend to be more broad and wide-ranging and could, for example, cover a marketing strategy, a manpower planning strategy or shareholder value strategy.

- **Policies**
Again, as with strategies, policies tend to be broad statements which are there to help managers at all levels within an organization to have some sort of direction about which way they are to proceed in carrying out their own responsibilities effectively, being aligned with the overall direction of the business itself. Examples of such policies could be a recruitment policy, credit policy and a people development policy.

- **Procedural plans**
These types of plans tend to vary in detail, although they will always indicate a number of things that need to be done, possibly in a particular way, during a

particular event or when undertaking a particular role or task. Generally, procedural plans become more frequent, more detailed and depended upon lower down the organization. This type of plan is very useful when a business unit is looking to maximize efficiency, in (for example) a production line type of environment where a particular task needs to be done only in a particular way, when trying to help people within a business become familiar with what needs to be done and how a task needs to be done, and when (perhaps across various business sites or departments spread across a wide geographical area) standardization of work is essential.

- **Programmes**

In this situation, there would tend to be a number of plans which are co-ordinated to become an overall programme. An organization may well have a programme to achieve a particular objective, for example, to train all its people in a particular skill, or depict them in a particular way or cultural change, or to refurbish all its offices throughout the whole business. Clearly an exercise like this would involve many smaller plans, or sub-plans, all of which need to be coordinated (which in itself can be quite a complex process).

- **A budget plan**

This type of plan is one that is a formal statement of expected financial results over a period of time, presented in numerical terms and monetary values. These days cost is a crucial factor in determining whether a business unit will do something, or be able to do something now and in the future. Therefore, some budgetary plans go into extensive detail to ensure that any budget that has been agreed is not overspent and concurrently that any money allocated to a particular business unit or project is used in the most effective way.

1.4
Why Plans May Not Work

So far we have looked at some of the key elements of planning in theory, and like many aspects of management, it all looks relatively straightforward on paper or in theory! Planning is one of many managerial functions that needs to be applied in the real world, and you will come up against many challenges when a theoretical plan is put into practice. The types of issues that could be faced will include the following:

- *For a plan to happen and to have a chance of being implemented successfully, it must have been designed or put together after the appropriate level of research has been undertaken. Any plan that is created without the availability of all the* necessary facts, information and detail will be flawed from the very start. In reality some of you may well have been in the situation where you have not had this luxury to research because your line manager, for example, may have requested your thoughts and proposals of how to proceed to achieve a particular business objective, and a plan has had to be produced in a much quicker timescale than would normally be ideal. In addition, some of the information that is required as a crucial ingredient into preparing the plan may not have been available, or the people designing the plan may not have been aware that the information existed in the first place.

- It is very important that all managers, team leaders and members of staff within each team are aware of how the planning process can help them to undertake their roles and responsibilities more effectively. Levels of ignorance about the benefits of planning will clearly hinder the contributions of individual members of staff, at whatever level, towards either designing a plan or making a plan actually work.

- These days, many more organizations are involving their people in more aspects of the business' daily activities, and one of these key involvements is in the planning process itself. 'Best practice' in terms of the planning process is to involve as many people as appropriate, and to invite their input and contributions. This means that from the very start more people will feel involved, feel they have made a contribution to the plan, have a greater understanding of why the plan is there in the first place, feel some ownership towards the plan and be committed to it. If, in reality, not everybody can be involved in this way, those that have been involved will act as ambassadors and communicators of good news to their colleagues throughout the business.

- Alternatively, if a plan is 'imposed from above' there is much more likelihood that the objectives within the plan will be met with a degree of resistance, resignation, frustration and even less than total commitment.

- There could be some cultural issues that need to be considered and in this case will involve the way in which the planning process has been traditionally undertaken. As mentioned above, culturally many more organizations are encouraging, or empowering their people to be involved in, many more aspects of day-to-day business life, including the planning process. In some organizations plans that involve specific (sometimes non-negotiable!) targets may be seen to be imposed and there is a danger of a 'fear factor' or 'brain culture' creeping in as individuals or business units within the organization look for alibis just in case they should not meet their own targets or objectives. In this latter scenario, it may well be that the managers or team leaders have a plan or series of targets imposed on them, and their own personal feelings (which may reflect the more negative aspects) will be passed on, inevitably, to their teams.

1.5
The Budget Process

Essentially, a budget is a plan stated in financial terms, and usually indicates what planned income is expected to be generated over a period of time together with any expenditure that is anticipated or planned for over the same period. In addition, capital expenditure, if appropriate, is also included in a budgetary plan.

The budget process itself includes the following:

- *Preparation of the budget.*
- *Agreement of the proposed budget with the appropriate parties (line management, senior executives).*
- *Planning the scope of the budget.*
- *Checking the budget in progress against planned income generation and expenditure.*
- *Being aware of any deviations in the levels of income generation or expenditure.*
- *Deciding whether any corrective action is necessary, to either increase income or reduce expenditure.*
- *On an ongoing basis compare actual budgetary performance with the planned budgetary expectations (known as budgetary control). This needs to be done on a continuous basis, as I am sure you are aware.*

A budget then can have many different purposes, some of which we shall consider below:

(1) A forecast budget

This is one that projects the future performance in financial terms of a business or organization. In the current business climate, forecasts of this nature are tending to be much shorter term, usually of around a year or less. One reason is the prevailing climate of rapid change and uncertainty over the longer term. In any case these forecasts need to be constantly reviewed, amended or even superseded.

(2) Allocating resources

This is where, either at an organizational level or more locally within a particular business unit, decisions are taken as to how much of a particular resource is required, available, and made available. Types of resources to be allocated include people, premises and finance. Again in the current business climate, all aspects of resource allocation are looked at extremely closely, and are often available in decreasing supply and the maxim to get 'more from less' is one that is often applied in terms of resource allocations. To allow organizations to retain overall control over resource allocation, or to ensure that ultimately they achieve their various targets in these respects, individual business units within an organization may be given targets or maximum levels of resources that they are allowed to use over a given budgetary period (probably one year).

(3) As a performance measure

Having a budget, in purely financial terms or in broader resource terms, is a very useful control mechanism for an organization or for individual managers or team leaders. The budget itself can be used as a monitor to indicate where levels of expenditure or even generation, for example, are 'on track' or alternatively are not going according to plan. This then gives the organization as a whole or members of the management team the opportunity to take any remedial action.

(4) As a target

A budget can also be used as a target and in some ways a motivational tool to help managers or teams within an organization to achieve or attain particular levels of performance. Arguably this would be more effective in a sale culture where particular levels of income generation would be expected to be achieved, or exceeded.

Unit 2

Organization

An organization is a very complicated and complex social system and the level of this complexity is partly determined by the organization's size. Within each organization, nevertheless, we have a situation where its employees are brought together to collectively achieve the business objectives of the organization itself. It therefore follows that an organization will provide the opportunity for individuals to achieve something on a collective basis that they could not possibly achieve in isolation.

An organization may exist for many reasons and purposes, including financial, educational, political, military, social – and I am sure you can think of additional ideas as well. What is also clear is that not all organizations are the same, in terms of size, what they do, how well they perform, how long they survive, and their impact on other organizations.

2.1
Formal and Informal Organizations

There is often a distinction made between the formal and informal organization, and we shall consider each of these in turn:

(a) **Formal organizations**
This is a type of organization that is formed with a purpose to achieve specific business goals. All businesses, then, are formal organizations.

Some key features of a formal organization include:

- *A clear and well-defined structure.*
- *Most key areas of conduct being defined by rules and regulations.*
- *Areas of responsibility being clearly defined.*

(b) Informal organizations

These are more spontaneously formed organizations, which may be created as a result of some common interests among various people or a planned gathering due to some particular sets of circumstances.

Characteristics of an informal organization include:

- *A tendency to be very flexible and adaptable.*
- *Having no particular structure or formation.*
- *Members will drift in and drift out on an informal basis.*

In reality, within every formal organization (a business), there are inevitably informal organizations. I have no doubt that you will be part of many informal organizations. For example, if you go to the pub on a Friday lunchtime, or if you play five-a-side football after work or if you go shopping together you briefly join an informal organization each time. An informal organization can sometimes also have more direct links to the achievement of business objectives, particularly when an informal group gets together and looks at how to get something done in what they see as a better way.

Furthermore, an informal organization may evolve when the formal aspects of an organization are not providing individual employees within that formal structure with enough 'satisfaction'. An informal structure may develop as a result to give individual employees a chance to develop in a social way or influence others and develop relationships in a way that they do not have the opportunity to do within the existing formal structure. Also, in (bit larger and more bureaucratic) formal structures they may be seen by their employees as inefficient, cumbersome and inflexible. It may be, then, in practical terms that an informal structure will (even has to) develop to maximize the business's potential to achieve its objectives. In this scenario, with the informal structure effectively operating 'underneath' or 'alongside' the formal structure, the informal structure will try to facilitate better communication and flows of information, and try to operate on a more streamlined basis.

You will probably realize that an informal organization can either be supportive or against the formal organization structure. The existence of a 'grapevine' implied in an informal system can improve communication, either for the good or otherwise of the formal communication structure. Also other possible dangers of the existence of an informal structure include:

- *Individual employees may see their contribution to the informal structure as being more important (and enjoyable!) than their supposed priority of working as part of the formal structure.*
- *A flourishing 'grapevine' not only implies that the official and formal*

communication strategy is ineffective, but also leads to rumour, incorrect messages and possibly individual employees becoming unsettled as a result.

- *Even within the informal structure, there may be loosely defined objectives which not only take time away from individuals focusing on the business objectives, but also may hinder the achievement of the overall organizational objectives.*
- *It is possible that an informal structure will undermine the role, position and influence of the formal management structure. One way in which this may happen is that the informal structure may include individual employees but exclude members of the management team.*

2.2
Organizational Objectives

In the previous section we have seen that an (informal) organization exists to achieve particular business objectives. An objective, then, is a target or goal that initially the organization as a whole looks to achieve. These objectives can be short-, medium- or long-term and tend to flow logically from the overall organizational mission statement (which in itself is a more global statement of what the organization exists for).

Beginning with the mission statement, this tends to be very general and may include statements like 'to be the best in their chosen market', or to 'maximize shareholder value'. It would be a useful exercise for you to find out what your own organization's mission statement is. From these more strategic aims, more specific organizational objectives then evolve. Typically, these organizational objectives involve:

- *The profitability of the organization.*
- *Overall clarity of what the organization expects from its employees.*
- *Obtaining maximum benefit from available resources.*
- *Productivity levels.*
- *Its planned place in the market in which it operates.*

Clearly, having these organizational objectives in place will not ensure their achievement in isolation. The objectives need to be cascaded throughout the organization, and at all levels.

This means that each part of the organization, and at each level throughout the organization, has its own set of objectives to strive for – the collective achievement of these more local objectives throughout an organization will mean that the organization overall will have fulfilled its (annual?) objectives. This cascade means that, beginning with the mission statement, regional or area objectives will be agreed and then more local (business unit or section) objectives will be derived and then finally these will be evolved to a more personal and individual level. At this final stage, every individual employee should have an agreed set of personal objectives, targets and priority areas which he or she clearly understands, and will therefore know what to do to play a part in the overall success of the organization itself.

Logically, objectives become more specific the lower down the organization we look; they may also become more short-term. In any case, throughout the organization, and at all levels, objectives and priority areas upon which to focus should be visible and clearly communicated (preferably being discussed and agreed beforehand) and these objectives, at whatever level, should be clearly seen to link with the higher and overall organizational objectives. These days, the achievement of objectives and targets is incentivized, with in many cases the incentives forming a major part in each individual employee's overall reward and recognition package.

We have seen elsewhere in this book the mnemonic 'SMART' objective and there are some useful guiding principles to follow there. Further, throughout the organization team leaders or managers should ensure that they themselves, and their teams, know exactly what they need to do. Throughout, again at all levels within the organization, collective success is facilitated if everybody's contribution is being continually monitored, reviewed and amended as necessary to ensure that staff maximize their chances of meeting their objectives and targets at the end of the year. Regular feedback to individuals throughout an organization to let them know how they are performing, and to receive guidance, is essential.

Some of the main advantages of having these objectives or targets throughout an organization include:

- *All employees having a clearer sense of purpose and direction.*
- *Motivational.*
- *The coordination and harmonization of individual efforts and activity.*
- *The opportunity for an organization to recognize individual and team contributions to the achievement of the overall objectives.*
- *Maximizing the opportunities for the business as a whole to achieve its strategic objectives.*

2.3
Organizational Structures

Organizational structures exist to illustrate lines of responsibility, authority, communication channels, and (working) relationships between individuals at all levels. These structures are there to successfully achieve all of this, although doing it in reality is often a lot more challenging than in theory!

As a general rule the bigger the organization the more complex the structure becomes, and this implies an immediate danger. This danger is that the more complex the structure is, the more bureaucratic and inflexible it can become – in this scenario, an organization may not be able to change direction as quickly as it needs to, or make decisions as quickly as would be ideal. This then means that any organization should adopt a structure that would appear to be the most appropriate to its own needs and purposes. Comparisons between a large organization and a small organization, or a public organization and a private company will clearly illustrate significant differences in their structures.

An organizational structure is often illustrated by an organizational chart or organogram. This gives a clear picture of what the organization looks like and includes features like:

- *Any hierarchy or change of command.*
- *Whether a system of one reporting line or matrix management exists.*
- *How an organization is split up into various departments or sections.*
- *How many levels of hierarchy exist.*
- *What spans of control are in place.*
- *How staff are organized across the whole organization.*

Within these structure charts, it becomes easier to see distinctions between what are known as 'tall' and 'flat' organizations. As you would anticipate a 'tall' organization has a management hierarchy with many layers of management between top and bottom with smaller rather than larger spans of control. A 'flat' organization tends to have fewer levels in the hierarchical range and within each level wider spans of control. One of the main trends of changes in organizational structures over recent years has been to 'de-layer', which means effectively layers of middle management have been removed which gives flatter organizations with their implied wider spans of control at each level of management. Try to think of some examples of 'tall' and 'flat' organizations.

Small Organizations

In a smaller organization, clearly the need for a structure is very different to that in a larger organization. Greater flexibility of each of its employees is implied and a smaller organization is often run by a smaller group of people or even one person. It may be that the people running the smaller organization are involved in most if not all of the key activity of the business, which means that any hierarchical structure becomes less critical. It therefore follows that a smaller organization may be able to be more flexible and adapt to change more easily, whereas a more formal and rigid structure would be a hindrance in this respect, making response times slower and adaptability more difficult.

In a smaller organization instead of a hierarchy, it is possible that every individual or team leader has a direct link into the 'top' of the organization. Everybody may know each other, and work collectively because in practical terms it is easier to do this. What growth in the size of an organization inevitably implies, however, is greater formality in structure, systems and procedures. The bigger the organization, the less likely (and impossible) is the reality that one person or a small team of people is involved in every aspect of the business on a personal level. This means that growth will bring a necessity at some stage to appoint a new team of other managers, and delegating specific areas of responsibility, authority and spans of control to them. Immediately, then, this new level of managers creates a hierarchy and further growth in the organization will imply new layers appearing in the hierarchy. Arguably, then, a small organization will change from being very flexible, to being much more formal, bureaucratic and inflexible in structure as it gets bigger and more complex.

Types of organizational structures

(a) **Functional structure**
In this type of structure, the functions for generic activities are put together to form a particular business unit within the organization as a whole. This functional segmentation is often evident at the higher levels of an organization and includes marketing, personnel, production, finance and so on. An illustration of a possible functional structure can be seen in Figure 2.1.

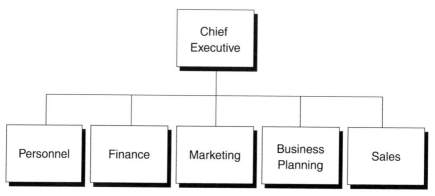

Figure 2.1

This principle of functional structures can be evolved to incorporate a line structure. This means that throughout the whole organizational structure every job holder (other than the Chief Executive or person at the top of the organization) reports (upwards) to only one person. In addition, the job holder in one particular position has the authority to manage all of those who are 'below' him or her involved in the same function.

Using the diagram below, this means that the head of personnel, for example, reports directly into the Chief Executive (one report). Conversely, the Chief Executive, using this diagram, has five direct reports. Finally, the head of personnel is responsible for all of those who work within the personnel function.

Other ways in which an organizational structure can be segmented could be along product lines, on a geographical basis or even according to the type of customers the organization serves across various market segments.

The structures that we have outlined above, so far, are all relatively simple and clearly segmented. In reality, this may not be either possible or, in fact, the case that exists.

(b) Matrix structures

We have seen in a functional structure everybody has only one boss or manager and, in theory at least, this should keep conflicts of interest to a minimum. Sometimes, however, that type of structure may be less than fully efficient and cooperation and coordination across a business may not occur with maximum effect.

In some cases, a matrix structure arrangement is necessary whereby individuals within a team effectively report to more than one manager. This may typically be the case in a project scenario when every member of the project team retains a line relationship with his or her own manager, although for the duration of the project effectively has another reporting line through to the project manager.

In itself this type of arrangement can be more complex for the following reasons:

- *Different sections automatically come into competition with each other for resources.*
- *There may be more conflicts on priorities, between those of the particular departments and those of the project teams.*
- *Who actually, in practice, is the boss of each member of the project team?*
- *This whole situation could become even more complex if an individual is seconded from his or her longer-term role to work on more than one project at any one time!*

So while the functional managers can feel that they are being pulled in (too many) different directions at the same time, a matrix approach can, when it works well, be more flexible – these days most organizations invest considerable time and resource in project management, so it is in everybody's best interests that this is in fact the case.

2.4
Culture

Culture is a word that is often used although for many is very difficult to define, primarily because of its complexity. Whyte and Plenderleith have defined culture as 'the way we do things around here' and the some of the key influences on what an organization's culture looks and feels like include:

- *The history of the organization itself.*
- *The size and scope of the organization.*
- *The impact and influence of technology.*
- *The purpose and objectives of the organization.*
- *The environment in which the organization operates.*

Think about your own organization and, using the criteria outlined above, think about any other criteria that could also apply, and try to evaluate and define your own organizational culture.

Charles Handy has produced much work on this area and has argued that there are four different types of culture, each of which we shall now look at.

Power culture

This type of culture is usually evident in smaller organizations and has one central power source. This central power source is influential throughout the organization, and is sometimes dominant. Everything that is undertaken throughout the organization is based upon expectations from the centre and because of the 'smallness' of the organization where this type of culture exists, red tape and bureaucracy are seldom seen as are roles and procedural activities.

As the name implies, in a power culture, individuals who held the key positions are the ones who exert most influence.

Handy illustrated the power culture in the form of a spider's web, as in Figure 2.2

Clearly, according to Handy, in a power culture the way and style of the organization itself is largely determined by the style and quality of leadership from the centre.

Role culture

Handy argued that this type of culture works primarily by rationality and logic. The type of organization that has a role culture typically has various functions, each with its own span of influence and control. Types of functions are personnel, marketing, sales, research and development, for example.

Handy illustrated this type of culture in the form of a Greek temple, as shown in Figure 2.3.

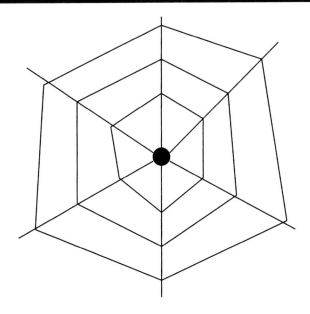

Figure 2.2

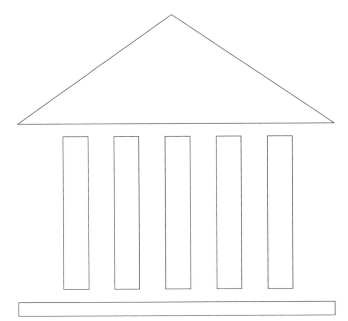

Figure 2.3

In a role culture, everything is coordinated by 'top management', including disputes and debates. In this type of environment, individuals tend to be placed in roles that suit their particular abilities and are asked to perform at a particular level and no more than this. A role culture is successful in a stable environment, which in reality in today's world is rare to find. Until recent years, examples of successful role cultures, primarily operating in a monopolistic or oligopolistic position in the marketplace, could be the Civil Service, oil companies and some of the larger retail banks.

In this type of culture, employees enjoy a high degree of job security and stability, and a predictable career development path.

Task culture

Handy argued that a task culture is one that is more job or project focused and illustrated it in a matrix format, as shown in Figure 2.4.

In this matrix the thicker lines indicate more pronounced roles for individuals and the key sources of power lies where these thicker lines intersect.

In this type of culture, Handy argued, expert power (having the appropriate skill and knowledge) is crucial and more important than position or personal power. All of the team is very important in a task culture and takes predominance over the performance of any one individual within a team.

A task culture must be adaptable and able to change very quickly, and this means that it may often be appropriate for a project environment, marketing activities, consultancies or advertising agencies.

Given the importance of the role of the team in this task culture, the challenge the top management faces is actually retaining ultimate control.

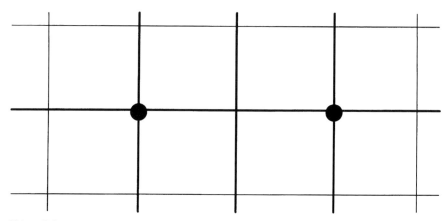

Figure 2.4

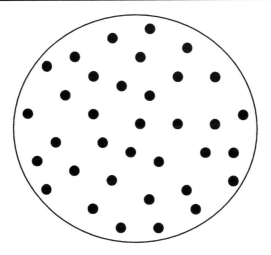

Figure 2.5

Person culture

Handy argued that in this type of culture, every individual is a central point of the organization and that the whole organization is there to 'serve' each individual employee. There is hardly any priority given to structural aspect and therefore in reality very few organizations can exist in this way in today's world. The obvious reason for this is that organizations exist to achieve objectives and because of the reasons we have discussed earlier this means that each individual will have his or her own objectives and targets, largely defined by the needs of the organization. Therefore the organization's needs will take predominance over those of the individual. The person culture can be illustrated as in Figure 2.5, in what Handy called a galaxy diagram.

In this type of culture, Handy argued, any type of control mechanism or managerial hierarchy is almost impossible because the organization is totally dependent upon each individual.

In today's world the only realistic possibilities in which a person culture could exist would be in a commune, a social group or perhaps a consultancy firm.

Unit 3

Control

Control can be seen as the way in which the ongoing activities of a business unit and the individuals within it are monitored in such a way to ensure that these ongoing activities fall in line with the overall objectives of the business plans. Control is a crucial management skill and is necessary because of the unpredictability of the future, and there is some inevitability about actual performance deviating at some stage from what was planned and expected. The control element aims to enable a business unit to adapt to such changes and to cope with any amendments to a plan, hopefully on a more proactive rather than a reactive basis.

Examples of what needs to be controlled include quality levels, budgetary issues, and stock. It is fairly self-evident that effective control cannot take place without the availability of relevant and meaningful management information. Furthermore control is not an activity that can exist in isolation from other management activities. Control is one way to facilitate overall success while being part of a much bigger picture, and looking to continually improve an existing approach to ongoing managerial activities.

3.1
The Control Cycle

There are many different variations on what the control cycle looks like, and we shall look at one that has six stages:

- *Firstly, making a plan that clearly states what needs to be done and what is looking to be achieved over a given period of time. Clearly, without a plan or series of objectives there can be no element of control that is required.*

- The plan itself needs to be formalized and should include measures of performance (SMART objectives), targets or standards that are to be achieved.

- The plan then needs to be brought to life, with various people within an organization carrying out the activities as required by the plan. On an ongoing basis, activities and work levels need to be recorded, observed and tracked.

- Then what is actually being achieved needs to be compared against the objectives and targets within the plan. In terms of the control cycle, this stage is often called 'feedback' where in practice deviations between actual activity and planned activity are identified.

- When considering any deviations as identified above, a decision should then be taken as to what to do about them. It may be that some sort of action is necessary to ensure that actual performance aligns with planned performance, or perhaps no action will be taken. Clearly, the cost/benefit equation needs to be considered in detail prior to deciding what needs to be done.

- If a decision is taken to take remedial action, then this should be implemented as effectively as possible. It may be that if prevailing circumstances have changed, or the view is taken that the plan in itself is not robust, then the plan and the objectives and/or targets within it may need reviewing.

The control cycle can be illustrated as shown in Figure 3.1.

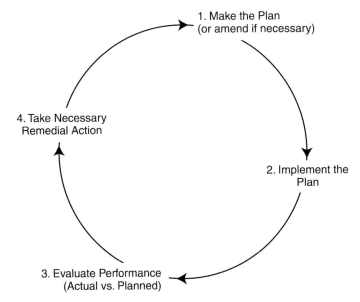

Figure 3.1

3.2
Effective Control Systems

For control to work effectively, and accepting fully that control is not a function that can work in isolation, we need to also be aware of the following issues:

(1) *An effective control system is largely dependent upon good planning. The plan should therefore contain clearly defined and realistic targets or objectives. Without this feature any control mechanism will not be able to effectively compare actual performance with planned performance in a meaningful manner.*

(2) *It needs to be very clear what parts of the plan are going to be controlled or monitored on an ongoing basis. This may involve some element of prioritization and any decisions of this sort need to be agreed beforehand.*

(3) *With the ongoing monitoring of actual performance against planned performance, ideally it should be agreed what level of tolerance or what variation is acceptable. There may be an error rate, margin of tolerance, number of breakages and so on which may deem to be acceptable. This decision will be based largely on the deviations within these margins and may be less than cost effective to do anything about.*

(4) *An effective control system is very clear about what needs to be done with the information comparing actual performance against planned performance. It is all very well collating all of this information, but it needs to be collected with a purpose and probably by somebody specific within the organization or business unit.*

(5) *It has to be agreed with what regularity this monitoring and control needs to be carried out. There will be examples when it needs to be carried out on an ongoing basis, and other examples when weekly or quarterly reviews could take place. The regularity and timing of the review process firstly needs to be agreed with all interested parties, and secondly needs to be appropriate for the particular case being considered. The timing of when information is made available can be very important, primarily because if information is received too late then it may be too late to do anything about any deviation from the plan. Ideally, the information needs to be made available so that proactive remedial action can be taken.*

(6) *The right type of control system needs to be in place appropriate to the particular activity that is being monitored. Technology has been a wonderful asset in many respects, although in reality it can be very expensive. Clearly, any control system needs to be cost effective, and to take an extreme example it would be obviously unwise to invest in a computerized control system that was to cost more than the actual profits generated from the achievement of the plan in the first place!*

3.3
Management by Objectives

Essentially, management by objectives (MBO) is a system that looks to both meet the needs of an organization to maximize profit and growth while enabling all its managers and team leaders to make a well-defined contribution, at the same time developing themselves to their full potential.

The starting point for an MBO system is to be clear about what the objectives in an organization are. This involves asking some fairly basic questions like:

- *What type of business do we currently operate in?*
- *What are the strengths and weaknesses of our business?*
- *What sort of (brand) image does the organization portray?*
- *What are the key competitors up to?*
- *What is the medium- and long-term plan?*

These types of issues will be debated at senior management executive level and then an organization can look at the objectives for managers at a senior level in the organization. Once these have begun to be clarified, then objectives can be discussed for managers at the lower levels within the organization.

Within the MBO system, the objectives that are agreed (note the emphasis on agreed) for managers at all levels of an organization will have some areas that are more important, or more of a priority to achieve, than other areas. The particular objectives are known as key result areas. This concept has the one main advantage of enabling managers to know where their (short-term) focus needs to lie. One possible disadvantage is that these key result areas are most likely short-term goals, and it should be ensured that managers at all levels within the organization are also giving thought to the longer-term issues.

Under an MBO system the performances of managers at all levels within the organization are reviewed at regular intervals. At these reviews, particular focus is given to performance against the key result areas which should be discussed in as an objective way as possible. The primary purpose, then, of these reviews is to measure a manager's performance against these clearly defined standards, or key result areas. The MBO philosophy would say that these reviews are not there to be critical or to look at an individual manager's natural managerial style, or character make-up or general effectiveness. Obviously to make these periodical reviews as effective as possible, the manager's own line manager needs to regularly monitor and review their direct subordinate's performance, particularly in key result areas.

Some of the potential benefits of MBO include:

- *When all the regular reviews are amalgamated, the organization effectively gets an accurate 'performance review' of its achievements against key result areas.*

- With the whole scheme of MBO, each manager knows what he or she needs to be doing to maximize their own contribution to business performance.
- By implication, a successful MBO system recognizes that an effective management information system is in place.
- Another clear implication with a well run MBO system is that a well structured and multi-directional communication system exists across the organization at all levels of management.
- At a strategic level, the organization can see the combined strengths and development areas of the management teams at all levels.
- MBO means that managers at all levels need to be ensuring their own contribution, and that of their teams, while they focus on the key result areas. This means that managers at all levels will be involved in the decision-making process at the highest level of which they are capable. This in itself ought to facilitate an environment of proactive self-development for managers at all levels and also a culture in which effective delegation is critical.

Unit 4

Change Management

We all live in a world of uncertainty, where change is happening all around us and it is seen as inevitable that the rate of change is going to constantly increase. Some of these changes will be happening to us, and with other changes we may be able to exert some influence on them. With this second category, we may have the choice of whether to respond to the impending change or not, and either positively or negatively. Alternatively if the change is happening (inevitably) to us, then we have to adapt; we have no choice.

There is no doubt that change is a very individual thing. For each of us it means different things, and with each change we react in different ways. The way in which you and I cope with change, resist some changes and deal with different types of crisis, or accept innovation will be slightly different. We may feel differently, act differently, think differently, respond more quickly or more slowly. We may enjoy change or be petrified of it.

All of us have faced, and dealt with, many changes in our lives so far and if we were to look back, I suspect that we would see that we have coped with some significant changes even if, with hindsight, they would appear to have been coped with on an instinctive (and perhaps unstructured) basis.

4.1
The Change Curve

Figure 4.1 illustrates what is called the change curve and it is based upon work conducted by Elizabeth Kubler Ross.

Kubler Ross argued that this model can be applied to any type of change, whether positive or negative. She argued that we would go through the same eight-stage process.

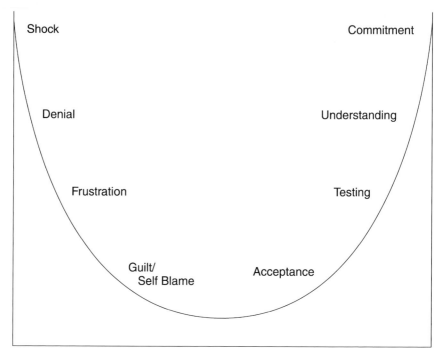

Figure 4.1

We shall consider each stage of the process in turn.

Shock

- *This occurs when an individual has to face any particular change, and is in fact in a state of shock. Typically people are not able to take it all in, and may often find themselves in a state of disbelief.*

Denial

- *At this stage an individual may well reject the change. People may try to create a scenario in their own mind where they refuse to believe that the change is happening or is about to happen at some stage in the near future. Here, an individual in 'denial' tries to look for evidence to confirm that this particular change will not happen; this is clearly impossible, and naive. This means that inevitably the individuals concerned will have to face up to the **fact** that the change **is** going to happen. Towards the end of this stage in the change process, the reality of the change being inevitable and unavoidable begins to dawn.*

Frustration

- *At this stage an individual is still in part-denial that the change is going to take place. This is particulary true when a change is happening to somebody; an individual at the 'frustration' stage feels particularly disappointed about his or her inability to influence what is happening. Quite often, an individual looks for somebody else to blame for the change that is about to occur.*

Guilt/Self blame

- *At this stage some individuals have real difficulty because they feel particularly helpless. They look around, maybe seeing colleagues coping really well with the change, or apparently coping really well, while they feel quite helpless and inadequate.*

Acceptance

- *This clearly a crucial stage in the change curve and will mean different things for each individual. After the previous period of possible helplessness, and feeling really down about the impending change, this stage starts to draw to a conclusion. According to this model, at some point in time an individual starts to believe that things just cannot get any worse than they already are. He or she begins to feel that even if the change that is to follow does happen, then things cannot possibly be more awful than they are already. Eventually, an individual begins to consider a new way forward, starts to forget the old attitudes or ways of working and actually begins to accept the reality that they may not be appropriate any more. At this point it is accepted that the only way forward it to try and come to terms with the impending change.*

Testing

- *Have begun to accept the inevitable, individuals begin to 'buy in' to the change and begin to feel a little more positive about it all. It may be that individuals will try out the new practices, behaviours or whatever else the change implies. Eventually, then, an individual really does start to feel good about the changes he or she faces.*

Understanding

- *The rate of acceptance of the change really begins to accelerate here and individuals begin to gain their understanding of changes, accept what this means to them personally and realize that the full involvement with, and commitment to, the change is unavoidable.*

Commitment

- *At this eighth stage in the model an individual has taken on the change. The implications of the change have been accepted fully and essentially become a part of what is now done every day.*

The model we have discussed can also be broken down into four main stages, as follows:

(1) Denial

As we have seen, this occurs where an individual thinks that change will never happen to him or her. The impending change will have no impact whatsoever. Furthermore whatever change is about to happen, people do not see it as anything new because they have been through many similar occurrences before. For many, in the denial stage, they try to ignore any change and try to carry on in a 'business as usual' manner.

Clearly as a team leader you need to be aware of how each of your team members is feeling as he or she faces up to change. You may have had the responsibility for managing change in your own business unit and if you have done so, then you will realize that there are several things that you can do to help members of your team cope.

Some ideas include:

- *Be aware of any aspects of denial by members of your team.*
- *Try to identify what problems, issues, and concerns members of your team feel that they are facing.*
- *Communicate regularly and clearly to your team about the change. This may mean holding regular meetings to clarify what the change is about and possibly having one-to-ones with each of your team members as required.*
- *Team leaders should also be showing empathy towards members of their team. It may be that they have more experience of dealing with and coping with change than their team members. They should therefore remember how they felt, and perhaps how their team members may be feeling at the moment.*
- *The team leader should be aware that each of their team will be coping with the change in a different way and therefore each individual team member needs handling differently.*
- *A crucial role for the team leader is to appear positive throughout any impending change. The team will look to the team leader for leadership and direction, as well as motivation and inspiration that everything will be alright.*

(2) Resistance

At this second stage, team members may feel and may in fact be acting in a more negative way. These feelings could well be illustrated by negative body language, members of the team acting defensively and, in extreme cases, perhaps individual team members trying to block, or delay (sabotage!) the impending change. The team leader needs to be aware of the 'grapevine' which can be a powerful way to find out what the true feelings towards the change are. Some of the team may be feeling that they have too much to do without coping with any more change and they will blame the business or the team leader on a more local basis, for the fact that the change is even being talked about.

In your role as team leader there are many actions that you can consider:

- *Make sure that you know what the 'grapevine' is saying.*
- *Continue your approach, throughout, of communicating effectively about what the change is, why it is happening, and what it will mean. Messages must continually be reinforced on either an individual or collective basis, or both.*
- *As with the 'denial' stage you need to be fully aware of how each individual member of your team is feeling and behaving. You will clearly need to identify as soon as possible any potential 'saboteurs'.*
- *Following on from the above point, as team leader you could, and should, identify your potential allies who actively welcome and sponsor the change. Their support for you in the time leading up to and during the change will prove invaluable.*

(3) Exploration

It is at this stage people begin to consider what options they actually face with the impending change. Their outlook will change as their curiosity levels increase as (inevitably) they look to find out more about what is happening or about to happen. They begin to feel more able to experiment, and eventually to accept the possibility that because the change is going to happen in any case, they may as well get used to the idea.

For a team leader, the timing of this 'exploration' stage is crucial – once reached the opportunity must be taken to drive the change forward. Some of the proactive things the team leader could be doing include:

- *Ensure that each member of the team plays a full part in the change itself.*
- *Try to encourage all members of the team to put forward ideas to help facilitate the change.*
- *Continue with the efforts towards effective communication throughout as has been done at the 'denial' and 'resistance' stages.*
- *In essence, at this stage the team leader is looking to empower the team to generate their own energy to accept the change.*

(4) Commitment

At this final stage, members of the team clearly take responsibility and ownership for the change, and actively begin to contribute towards making the change a success. It is now that individual team members look for ways to make the change work even better, to submit ideas on continuous improvement and to really commit themselves to this change.

For some, they could look back with hindsight and say 'what an earth was all the fuss about', although for others they will have been through quite a torturous process which has finally led to them accepting the change. As ever the team leader's role is absolutely pivotal and some primary activities at this fourth stage of this model are:

- *A celebration of success to mark the fact that the team have incorporated the change into their daily activities.*
- *To recognize, as (if) appropriate, individual team members for their contributions towards making the change a success.*
- *Even at this stage, there is no way that the team leader can relax, in terms of the change process itself. A positive approach to now implementing the change and seeing it work in reality, and sustaining the implied activities from the change, are still high on the agenda. This means the team leader will always need to be monitoring progress and recognizing individual contributions.*
- *At some point in the future, depending on the particulars of each change, the team leader will need to evaluate how the change was incorporated into the work activities. This review process will help to identify what areas, if any, could possibly be done differently next time, and to understand what lessons can be learnt.*

This simple change process can be illustrated as in Figure 4.2.

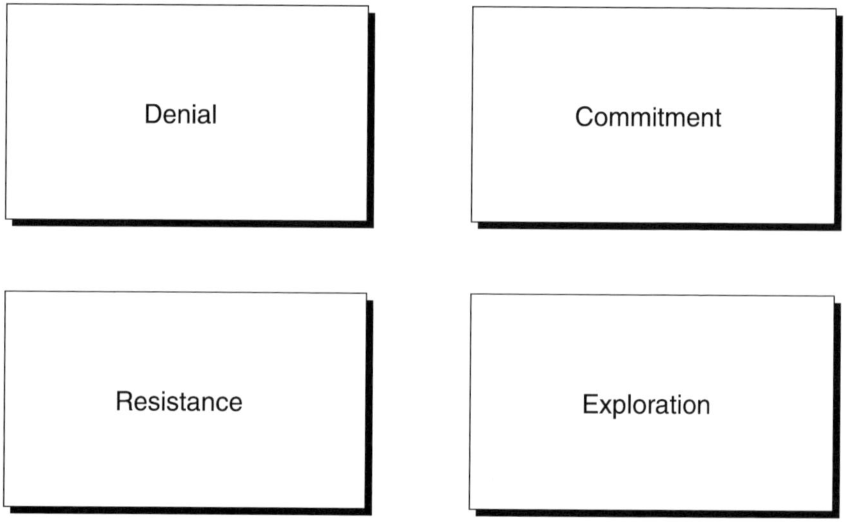

Denial

Commitment

Resistance

Exploration

Figure 4.2

So far then, we have looked at two theoretical models of how change works. You will have already gathered how complex change is, and yet it is a continuous phenomenon that we are facing every day. Change is here with us, both in our working and domestic lives. Whichever way we consider change, there is no doubt that it is inevitable.

4.2
Managing Emotions Through Change

The way we feel as team leaders, and how our team leaders feel throughout change is obviously a very important issue. When the 'old habits' are put to rest, for some this will mean sadness, and possibly even a feeling of regret or loss. For some, they will be changing habits or practices that they have been doing for years and that by accommodating change they may feel threatened or frightened – there is a real possibility that some members of your team will feel undervalued, and that their own skills and competencies are now no longer relevant or appreciated.

Sometimes during the change process feelings and emotions can be at different extremes. One possibility is a feeling of isolation and loneliness. Another possibility is one of excitement and not being able to wait until the new change arrives. These ranges of feelings will affect all of your team members in different ways and to different extents, and will be evident and prevalent while the change process itself is underway.

4.3
Why Change Can Fail

We have already mentioned that for some, they see no need to change, primarily because they see nothing wrong with the way things are. It is often seen as the easy option to maintain the 'status quo'. Some people will go to great extents to avoid what they see as the pain and upset of any change.

Undoubtedly, any team of individuals will not move forward **together** until every team member is absolutely clear about what the objectives of the change are and what exactly the benefits of the change will be. Again we need to reinforce the importance of you as team leaders being aware of how each of your team members will be feeling and how they are likely to respond to change – ultimately it is you who will have the responsibility for successfully managing the change.

Change may fail for some of the following reasons:

- *Where there is a basic misunderstanding about what the change actually is.*

- *That the change itself is not prepared for adequately and insufficient planning and preparation takes place beforehand.*
- *Throughout the change process there are at least some of the team who remain unclear as to where they are trying to get to.*
- *Change being seen as a 'quick fix' and not the longer-term complex process that it is.*
- *Inadequate communication of the change.*
- *Where change focuses retrospectively rather than towards the future, where it should be.*
- *Employee resistance.*
- *Inadequate training for yourself as team leader and your team members.*

4.4
Reasons for Change

Change can come about for many reasons, and we can categorize these under the following broad headings:

- **Economic**

For example – competitive pressures, pressure from employees, pressure from prevailing economic circumstances.

- **Social**

For example – change in tastes, change in fashions, the role of women in the workplace, the trend towards full equality, increasing awareness of 'global warming'.

- **Political**

For example – change of government, new legislation (e.g, Union law, health and safety at work, consumer protection).

- **Technological**

For example – the introduction of the paperless office, industrial robots, journeys into space, revolutions in transport systems.

Generally, most of us in the human race like some form of continuity and change is not something most people would actively seek.

In the workplace change can bring many benefits. Examples include:

- *Change can bring a new interest to your job.*
- *Change could open possibilities for future career development.*
- *Change can provide the opportunity to learn new skills.*
- *Change will provide you with a new challenge.*

As a 'golden rule' the more involved managers or team leaders are in the change itself, the more support and encouragement they can give to their team leaders as they face up to change. In some ways we can say that it is not the change itself that causes so much anxiety and potential upset, it is more the uncertainty about what the change is and what it will mean in the future.

When planning for change, there are many things to be thought about and these include:

- *Why are we changing?*
- *What are the objectives of the change?*
- *Who is involved in the change?*
- *What constraints may be faced?*
- *What is the (hopefully realistic) timescale we have to implement the change?*
- *What resources are available to help facilitate the change itself?*
- *How will the 'business as usual' scenario be affected during change?*

Having reviewed some of the key features that will be evolved in the planning process itself, as a team leader, possibly together with your team in a 'brainstorming' exercise, you may move on to consider the implication of all of these. Some of the questions you may come up with are:

- *What will be the (implied) changes in your team's working practices?*
- *What training requirements are there for you as team leader and for your team?*
- *What additional communication needs to take place?*
- *How will the team collectively be affected?*
- *How will each individual member of the team be affected?*
- *Will any other groups or business units or parts of the organization be affected?*
- *What are the possible (probable) reactions to the change likely to be?*
- *Are there any cost implications?*
- *What are the realistic timescales to introduce the change?*

These are some of the main issues; no doubt you and your team will be able to think of some more.

Unit 5

Communication

As with many of the other areas we are looking at in this book, communication is also difficult to define. Most definitions will include words such as: exchanging information, sharing information, transferring ideas between two or more people, for example. We can, however, draw out some generic features from whichever definition we choose to use, as follows:

- *Communication always involves a 'sender' and at least one 'receiver'.*
- *Communication occurs when a message is shared or transferred between at least two people.*
- *Communication is always a two-way process because any transfer or sharing of a message results in some kind of response (from the 'receiver').*

Some of the basic skills of communication, which I am sure you are aware of, are: speaking, writing, behavioural and listening. We shall explore what these skills actually imply a little later in this section.

As an exercise it may be useful for you to complete the following table to identify clearly which means of communication you use while carrying out some of your main responsibilities.

Management Skills	Verbal	Written	Behavioural	Listening
Establishing and maintaining good working relationships.				
Providing information to line management.				
Allocating duties to your team members.				
Preparing and processing management information				
Receiving suggestions and ideas from your team members about ways to improve any aspect of the workplace.				
Providing training for existing and new team members.				
Managing any conflicts or disputes.				
Holding meetings with colleagues, or customers (internal or external).				

Which particular communication skill you use for each management skill identified above will vary according to the details of the case that you are considering. Also, when you are applying the same skill, although in different circumstances, it may be that you require to apply different aspects of communication.

An example occurs when you are required to provide management information to your boss. Sometimes a written paper is necessary, especially if a permanent record is required or if there is much detail to pass on. Alternatively, there may be times when a brief oral up-date is adequate.

The grid above, while fairly simple and quick to complete, can be useful. One idea is to ask your peers to also complete this grid and to compare any differences between your own approach and that of your colleagues.

5.1
A Theoretical Model for Communication

There are many variations on a theme here, because in diagrammatic form most communication models include three main dimensions: people, information, feedback. We can illustrate this concept as shown in Figure 5.1.

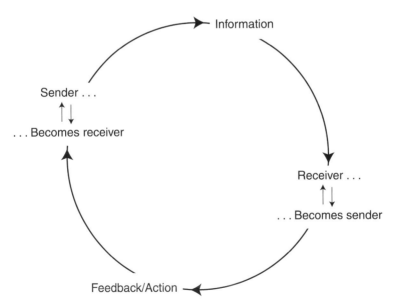

Figure 5.1

Looking at each of the three dimensions of this model in more detail:

(a) People

In any communication process there are a minimum of two people involved. Firstly, there is the person who sends the message, known as 'the sender'. Secondly, there is the person or people who are being communicated to, 'the receiver' or 'the receivers'. This sounds so easy, whereas in fact, as you will be only too aware, communication can become an enormously complex process. How two people communicate with each other can also be influenced by some of the following factors.

- *The personalities of the sender and the receiver.*
- *How both parties are feeling at the time of the communication. Their mood at that particular time will have a major influence on how that communication is undertaken.*
- *Personal feelings that the sender and receiver have towards each other.*
- *Existing levels of knowledge of both the sender and receiver about what is being communicated.*
- *The culture of the business unit or organization in which the communication is taking place. As a result, the communication may be more formal or informal, although always in line with the prevailing culture and tradition of that organization.*

(b) Information

Information, using the model we have illustrated above, is what is being communicated. Other models refer to this dimension as 'the message'. The sender needs to be very clear about 'the message' before sending it. If you think that this is incredibly obvious, then try and remember how many communications you have received that are either unclear, incomplete, require translation, are inaccurate, may be misleading, perhaps containing untruths, arrive late, contain jargon . . . who said communication was easy!!

(c) Feedback

In reality any 'sender' does not know whether the 'receiver' has successfully received the communication or message unless he or she confirms that this has been the case. The receiver's response will provide that confirmation; it may also lead to a further course of action from the (original) sender.

So even in this brief overview, I am sure that you will now be convinced that communication is not only a crucial leadership attribute, it is also a considerable skill to master.

There are some barriers to effective communication and we shall outline some of these below:

(a) **Organizational culture**

This is an important influence on the way information is communicated. Culture can either facilitate communication, or it can be a major hindrance. If you work in an environment where information is shared informally, generally in a relaxed manner with open and free discussions to debate any issues, then you will be used to this approach. Alternatively you may be working in an organization that has a strong format. This will probably mean that communication is much more formal and follows a more rigid pattern. Therefore, in this type of environment, the way in which you would be expected to communicate would be much more clearly defined. For example, in some circumstances a memo would be expected, or a formal meeting held, and so on.

(b) **The work environment**

There may be some aspects of the work environment that make it difficult to communicate effectively. Examples include taking a confidential message by telephone in an open-plan environment or receiving a message when somebody is trying to have a conversation with you at the same time.

(c) **Authority and bureaucracy**

In some cases, effective communication is hindered because of the (unnecessarily) way in which it is expected to be undertaken. In some organizations there is a particular communication system that has to be followed. There may be a system that does, in fact, overcomplicate a fairly straightforward process. It may be that the message has to pass through several different parties before it reaches its intended destination (receiver). This may lead to the message itself becoming distorted in the transmission process.

(d) **Noise**

This method of communication is as it sounds. It can be described as any sort of noise which can cause the message being sent to be distorted, interrupted, difficult to hear, impossible to read. Obvious examples here could be telephones, traffic, workmen, machinery – this aspect can be particularly irritating!

(e) **The language used**

One golden rule of communication is to keep it as simple as possible. The longer the communication, the more likely it is that the key messages may be lost or points of emphasis missed. Similarly, communication should be as precise as possible and should not really contain jargon. When this first happens, as we mentioned earlier, it may be that the receiver will need a translator!

(f) **The feelings of those involved**

How the sender feels about the receiver and vice versa will have a major influence on how successfully any communication is carried out. Some times we hear what we want to hear, see what we want to see, read what we want to read – this aspect of human nature may in itself cause us to misunderstand a message or information. We need to be aware of how the sender is feeling and how the receiver is feeling, also what the ongoing working relationship is between both parties.

5.2
Becoming an Effective Communicator

Some of you will be more experienced than others at communicating and it is true to say that the more practice you get the more effective you should become. One main way in which you can become more effective at communicating is by planning the communication itself beforehand.

How you actually plan any communication will depend on some or all of the following:

- *Your own level of knowledge, and that of the receiver (if known).*
- *The consequences of communicating ineffectively with the receiver.*
- *The urgency with which the communication needs to take place.*
- *Your ongoing relationship (if you have one) with the intended receiver.*
- *How important this relationship is in terms of this communication.*
- *The complexity of the information that needs to be communicated.*

In any case, some guiding principles for you to consider before making any communication, which I hope you find helpful, are given below:

- *Why you are communicating in the first place.*
- *What it is you are intending to communicate.*
- *Who you are communicating with.*
- *What medium you will use to communicate.*
- *The timing of the communication.*
- *Where you should communicate.*

Sometimes it is useful to refer to the check list even if you have considerable experience in communicating, just to make sure that you are as effective as you think you are!

5.3
Communication Skills

If it was not clear before the beginning of this section, I have no doubt that you will be much clearer now that communication is a key management skill. We shall now move on to look at some of the main skills that need to be evident when communicating effectively.

(1) Listening skills

Listening skills are a very advanced faculty because they integrate the ability to concentrate, use effective body language, have good eye contact and focus your thoughts clearly.

During each working day all of us have many occasions when we have to listen, and some of the action points you may wish to pursue are:

- *Ask any questions if you need to seek clarity and check your understanding.*
- *Write down the message as you hear it.*
- *Make sure the communicator (sender) clearly understands what he or she means.*
- *Make sure that you do actually listen!*

Furthermore think about how the sender or communicator is feeling when you are listening to him or her. How would you feel if you were sending a message and the receiver looked blatantly bored, kept interrupting, started doing something else at the same time – it is not on, really, is it?

(2) Questioning skills

Effective questioning techniques mean that problem solving can be facilitated and any checking of understanding can be achieved.

There are two main types of questions that you need to be aware of.

An open question is one that deliberately invites a more detailed response. As such, an open question typically begins with why, how, who, what, where.

Alternatively, a closed question is much more direct, one where a simple 'yes' or 'no' answer is called for.

In reality, most of our communications, conversations or messages that we send and receive invite a range of questions, some open and some closed.

(3) Body language

This is another very complex area for us to briefly look at, and worthy of at least one book in its own right. As a listener we should be looking at the body language of a communicator (assuming he or she can be seen at the time of the communication) and we should be able to get a reasonably clear picture of the communicator's genuineness, confidence and actual interest in the message being conveyed. Some priority areas to focus upon are the communicator's eye contact, expression and posture.

Examples of positive body language include:

- *Good eye contact.*
- *A smile.*

- *A relaxed posture.*
- *Probably leaning slightly forward.*

Alternatively, some examples of a more negative body language include:

- *Poor eye contact.*
- *Crossed arms.*
- *The appearance of being tense.*
- *The body turned away from the other party.*
- *Slouching.*

Perhaps you will be able to remember occasions when either you personally, or somebody who has been communicating with you, has been saying one thing while their own body language has been conveying a totally different message!

(4) Your voice

How we use our voice portrays expression, emphasis, meaning and interest. The way in which our voices are used are a main factor in how effectively the attention of the receiver is achieved.

Our tone of voice should be appropriate and relative to what we are trying to say at that time. The tone of voice provides the receiver with some clear implications of your being either angry, sad, happy or persuasive. In most cases the tone of voice that the communicator (or sender) uses matches quite naturally and clearly the words that are being said.

(5) Awareness of how you come across

Another important area to consider and some features to include in your thoughts here are:

- *What you need to do to make a positive 'first impression' with the receiver on each occasion.*
- *Your personal appearance.*
- *Your personal posture.*
- *How effectively you use eye contact.*
- *How confident you appear.*
- *Your own personal mannerisms (if you are aware of them!).*

Each of us should ensure that the messages we project, in terms of our personal appearance and actions, are the ones that we want to project.

(6) Making your points effectively

We have already seen that it is very important to plan your communications. You then need to think about how you are going to gain the attention of 'the receiver'.

Timing may be crucial here, as just perhaps the very last thing on a Friday afternoon may not be the best time to hold an in-depth team meeting!

Every time that you make a communication you must speak clearly and in a concise and focused way. Try to be aware of how the receiver may be feeling at the time you are communicating – respond to their body language or any comments and/or objections that they may make.

If the length of the communication demands it, it may be sensible to include regular summaries while making your message. This gives the receiver regular opportunities to clarify any issues, and it helps you as communicator to ensure that your message is being received as planned.

We then need to ensure that any messages we have sent are appropriately received and understood. Some ways of doing this will include: being aware of the receiver's body language, asking questions, even repeating the message!

5.4
Methods of Communication

Of the multitude of communication media available, and will become increasingly available in the future, the most popular include:

- *Within groups, holding presentations, meetings or facilitating discussion groups.*
- *In writing by using newsletters, circulars or memos.*
- *By using 'informal' communication channels, like, for example, the 'grapevine'.*

Written communication is still the most frequently used communication medium and every time we write something we must always question the need to do so. Having done this our primary objective is then to earn the attention of the reader (receiver).

Some aspects of 'best practice' are:

(1) **Use plain and simple language.**
Use language that people can understand. Keep your sentences generally short and concise. Always try to use words that are shorter and understood by most people; at all costs avoid jargon. If you do need to use any technical words or phrases ensure that they are defined clearly.

(2) **Grammar**
Remember 'first impressions' do count – some 'receivers' still focus on a missing comma, an incorrect spelling or some other aspect of incorrect grammar, and actually miss out on the messages contained within the overall written communication itself!

Issues that will require due attention when considering grammatical aspects include: abbreviations, apostrophes, capital letters, commas, paragraphs, bullet points, spelling. Clearing none of us can expect to be word perfect and grammatical experts – nevertheless it is worth our time to make sure we get it as right as we possibly can. Sometimes you can spend a considerable amount of time working on a written document, and it would be a pity if it lost its impact due to some avoidable error. It may be helpful to ask a colleague or friend to read through the document as they will look upon it with 'fresh eyes'.

(3) Report writing

One of the many roles of a team leader and sometimes a team member is to be able to write a report, frequently for our line manager although sometimes for other purposes. These days there are so many pieces of paper working their way through any given business unit that it is important that any report that you do is one that gains priority in terms of having as good a chance as possible of being read. It therefore follows that a report needs to be as brief as possible, while being clear, focused and well presented.

In addition, when writing a report, there are some other areas to consider:

(a) Planning the report

This is where the author of the report needs to be very clear about what message or messages the report should contain and ultimately convey to its intended audience. Quite often, this means a report has some specific objectives which clearly identify what the target audience will have learnt, felt or be expected to do as a result of having read the report.

(b) The structure of the report

There are many options on how to format a report, although whichever method you choose needs to be appropriate to the particular report that is being written. In every case a logical and reader-friendly 'structure' needs to be achieved – a common approach is to have a report that contains a series of headings throughout, which facilitate the reader finding a way around the report itself. These series of headings should be accompanied by a numbering system which aids the indexing of the report.

(c) Contents of the report

'Best practice' indicates that formal reports contain the following:

- *A title page.*
- *A contents page.*
- *An executive summary.*
- *An introduction to the report.*
- *The main body of the report.*

- *Conclusions and recommendations.*
- *An action plan (if appropriate).*
- *Bibliography.*
- *Appendices.*

(d) Writing the report itself

The main areas to focus upon, some of which we have mentioned before, include:

- *Make sure you are aware of who your audience is.*
- *Always be clear and concise.*
- *Use clear language.*
- *Avoid jargon.*
- *Take care with your grammar and spelling.*
- *Use illustrations or graphics when possible.*
- *Take care with your presentation.*

5.5
Other Aspects of Communicating Across a Business Unit

We need to reinforce again that communication is a skill – it is something that we all have the opportunity to learn and to continually develop our skills throughout our career.

Hopefully you work in an atmosphere of open communication which means that any issues that affect your team or you as team leader are shared as soon as realistically possible. We all work in an environment of rapid change and that means that there will always be much to communicate, and some of this communication will be good news but by no means all of it will be. All communication that you undertake should always be honest, clear and not open to misinterpretation or misunderstanding.

(a) A proposed communication strategy

There is so much to communicate and unless the management of a particular business unit have some kind of plan about what should be communicated, by whom, when, and with what frequency, their best intentions will probably fail. A balance needs to be struck about the critical need for regular effective communication and over communicating – sometimes this can be very difficult to achieve, and your first attempt at planning your communication strategy may need to be amended as you learn what works and what does not work quite so well.

Examples of regular communications include:

- *Management meetings.*
- *Open forums held by management with a cross-section of staff from the business unit.*
- *Section head meetings.*
- *Social committee meetings.*

(b) Team meetings

Meetings are a part of our daily working life and seem to be the most popular way of keeping colleagues throughout a business informed about what is happening across their organization and in their specific workplace. Some of you may have been unfortunate enough to attend a meeting which, by the time it is completed, you wonder why you were there in the first place. Sadly, across businesses all over the world, this scenario occurs far too often. Every meeting that is held involves an investment of each attendee's time, and can involve considerable cost and opportunity cost.

A well-run meeting has the following features:

- *All agenda items are submitted well before the meeting itself (by an agreed date).*
- *For each item that is to be discussed at the meeting, there needs to be a clear sponsor and some very clear 'desired outcomes' to be gained from discussing the issue at the meeting.*
- *Circulating an agenda before the meeting.*
- *Ensure the meetings are held at a frequency that is appropriate to their purpose.*
- *Ensure any action points are agreed and then implemented by the agreed dates.*
- *Minutes and agreed action points should be recorded and then circulated to all attendees and those who were unable to attend.*
- *An appropriate venue (if available) should be used to hold the meeting, where hopefully you will not be interrupted except in an emergency.*
- *Once arranged, the meeting should be cancelled only as a very last resort.*

(c) Open forums

These sessions are where the team leader or unit manager meets regularly with the team to discuss any topical issues that are raised. One benefit of holding such sessions regularly is that open two-way communication, carried out in an environment of mutual trust and respect, becomes a reality.

Whoever is holding the open forum needs to ensure that everybody in attendance has the opportunity to make a contribution, as they wish, and to express any opinions that they may have. The facilitations skills of the manager or team leader are very important. Also to enhance the credibility of such an event any issues that are raised should be dealt with as soon as possible, with the appropriate feedback given to the team.

(d) Newsletters

Any newsletter that is available within your own organization, or one which you are thinking of producing yourself, should have content that will be of interest to your colleagues across the business unit. Any element of duplication compared with what is being communicated elsewhere must be avoided.

Internal newsletters seem to be increasingly popular and may contain some of the following features:

- *The manager's or team leader's column.*
- *Topical staff issues.*
- *Sport and social activities.*
- *Feedback from any open forums held.*
- *Competitions.*
- *Any charity events.*
- *Articles recognizing success.*

(e) The notice board

How often have you heard one of your team members or perhaps even yourself denying all knowledge of seeing a notice that has been displayed for some weeks! In reality, therefore, a notice can be a very effective way of endorsing and supporting any communication messages or issues that need to be conveyed. But it is probably unwise for any communication message to be conveyed solely by a notice.

Any notice board should not become a dumping ground and it needs to be ensured that all notices are relevant and not out of date. Generally, a notice should be displayed when it is used to pass on a message that affects a whole business unit.

(f) Responsibilities

I think we would all agree that ultimate responsibility for an effective approach to communication always rests with the unit manager or team leader. Nevertheless each and every one of us has some degree of responsibility for ensuring that the communication process is successful.

THAT ALSO MEANS YOU!

Unit 6

Leadership

There have been many views on what leadership is, and I am sure that you will have your own opinion. You probably know a number of people whom you personally consider to have been effective leaders for whatever reasons. When you consider some of the generic skills and abilities of these leaders I am sure you will find some similarities. We shall here be considering various aspects of leadership in terms of managing a team or a business unit.

Traditionally, a manager needs to be able to plan, organize, monitor and control, communicate, motivate and evaluate. We would hope that most team leaders have these abilities, and these days they are essential as a minimum to survive. However, you could also argue quite effectively that these skills are merely the start.

Other key attributes an effective leader and team manager needs to have include:

- *The ability to empower their team members.*
- *The ability to understand the importance of customer service (both internal and external).*
- *The ability to build effective working relationships with the team, managers, peers and other business units.*
- *Coaching skills.*
- *The essential skill of creating a working environment where the team enjoy coming to work, and are every day inspired to give of their best.*

I am sure you can add some more attributes that either you or perhaps your own line manager has.

In addition, there are many traits of an effective leader, and here are a few for you to consider:

- *Being consistent.*
- *Being genuinely interested in the team members.*
- *Being visibly loyal to the team during difficult times.*

- *Advanced listening skills.*
- *Having undoubted integrity.*
- *Being dependable.*
- *Always being fair.*
- *Recognizing success.*
- *Creating an environment of open and two-way communication.*

Again these are some ideas, and these lists will continue to grow as the expectations placed upon any team manager or leader continue to become greater and greater.

6.1
The Roles and Responsibilities of a Team Leader

I am sure you realize that each leader or team manager seldom has the chance to display one particular skill in isolation. Far from it, typically many roles have to be played at the same time. Over recent years there have been many theories and models put forward to try to categorize managerial behaviours and we shall consider those put forward my Henry Mintzberg and John Adair.

Henry Mintzberg proposed a view which believed that managers and team leaders' activities could be categorized into three main areas:

- *Interpersonal roles.*
- *Informational roles.*
- *Decisional roles.*

Mintzberg then went on to sub-divide these three categories even further, as follows:

- *Interpersonal*
  - Figurehead.
  - Leader.
  - Liaison.
- *Informational*
  - Monitor.
  - Disseminator.
  - Spokesperson.
- *Decisional*
  - Entrepreneur.
  - Disturbance handler.
  - Negotiator.
  - Resource allocator.

The interpersonal roles were those that primarily focused on managing people, that is the team. Mintzberg also believed that the team leader or manager needs to be seen by others to be fulfilling that role and to act as a figurehead. Similarly, managers need to be able to create the type of relationship with their team so that the team themselves look to the manager as their leader.

Mintzberg believed that the informational roles were those that focused on dealing with information flows inside and outside of the team leader's particular business unit. In today's working world, there is an infinite amount of information available to all of us and one crucial skill of any team leader is to be able to be clear what it is that is required, what is useful and what can add value to their own performance and that of their team. Once the appropriate information has been obtained, the team leader then needs to be able to manage it effectively – in other words to decide what to do with it. This involves the ability to prioritize the information that is available, and to communicate in an appropriate manner and with a realistic frequency relevant information to their team. In this way, using Mintzberg's words, a team leader will be acting as a 'disseminator'.

Decisional roles are clearly related to the decisions that refer to the work being undertaken in a particular business unit. Mintzberg saw the entrepreneurial role as being one where the team leader needs to proactively seek opportunities to maximize his or her own performance and that of their team when compared with appropriate competitors either internal or external. Any team leader is expected to deal with any issues that arise (often unexpectedly!) and maintain a 'business as usual' work performance throughout. Again using Mintzberg's words, the ability to be a 'disturbance handler' is essential! The ability to negotiate is also vital, which is where a team leader needs to have the ability to reach agreements as required to ensure that progress towards achieving business objectives is maintained. In this third part of Mintzberg's model, the ability to maximize the use of available resources is again identified as a key leadership skill. I have no doubt that we can all relate to this, in the current climate of often severe restrictions on resource availability in terms of premises, budget, people and machinery, for example.

6.2
John Adair

In one of his many books, *Effective Leadership*, Adair produced a model that identifies what he sees as the three main responsibilities of a team leader. This model is illustrated in Figure 6.1.

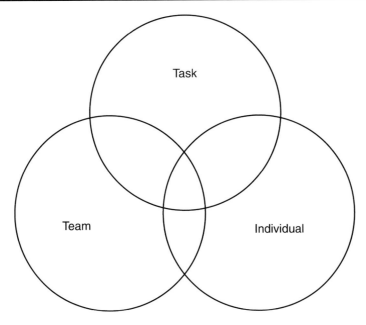

Figure 6.1

We shall look at each element of this model in turn.

The individual

Adair saw a team leader having some of the following responsibilities towards individual team members:

- *Providing ongoing support and encouragement.*
- *Ensuring that individual team member's abilities are used to the full, by allocating appropriate duties to undertake.*
- *Ensuring that each team member is aware of what his or her own responsibilities and objectives are.*
- *For each team member to be aware of how he or she is performing against work objectives by regularly assessing job performance.*
- *To give protection and guidance if required to any team member.*

The team

In Adair's view in the context of the team, a team leader is responsible for:

- *Showing visible commitment to the team at all times.*
- *Ensuring the team are aware of the collective objective and performance standards that they are expected to achieve together.*
- *Making sure that everybody is aware of their own individual role within the context of the team.*
- *Creating an environment where the team performance can be maximized.*
- *Always being there for the team, in the good times, and of course the bad times!*
- *Representing the team to higher management, and conversely representing higher management to the team.*
- *Liaising with other business units/teams or departments.*

The task

Clearly we can argue that the main reason for the existence of any team is the task that they are expected to do. In other words if the task was not there, quite possibly the team would not exist. There is a popular view which says that achievement of a task is the team leader's main responsibility, and therefore that all other considerations are secondary.

6.3
Finding Out What Happens in Reality

It is always an interesting exercise to compare theory with practice and we can look at and observe the various actions you take in carrying out some of the main responsibilities of leadership or effective management. You can also discover how (and if!) your own line manager carries out some of these functions. When doing your own self-review or observing your manager it is always more useful to use specific examples – this is because they help to focus your mind on being specific rather than vague when looking for actual evidence. You could, for example, use the grid shown in Figure 6.2.

Leadership Function	Specific Instances of your Own	Examples by Line Management
Setting/Agreeing Objectives		
Planning		
Organizing		
Motivating		
Controlling		
Delegating		
Leading by example		

Figure 6.2

STRENGTHS WEAKNESSES	
(What we know we can do well – and have the evidence to prove it)	(What we know we need to work upon – again having specific examples to work upon would be useful)
OPPORTUNITIES THREATS	
(What opportunities are available to help you to develop – this could be training, finding a mentor, obtaining a transfer)	(What may prevent you from succeeding and developing – could be cost constraints, possible redundancy, not having the support of your line manager)

Figure 6.3

Another way of completing a self-review is to undertake a SWOT analysis, which effectively looks at what you see as your attributes as an effective team leader and similarly in what areas you need to focus on in order to develop your skills. You can highlight your strengths and developmental areas using a chart as shown in Figure 6.3.

By completing a self-review like this you will be able to highlight what strengths you have, and what you need to work upon. Ideally, you could then produce your own action plan, which of course needs to be both realistic and achieveable and which will concentrate upon developing your strengths (i.e., making them even stronger) or focusing upon specific developmental areas. You may feel it appropriate to discuss your plans for self-development with your line manager.

Furthermore, there can be no doubt that the ultimate responsibility for fulfilling your own potential and self-development is yours. You therefore need to be proactive in doing this and it may be that completing regular and honest self-reviews, similar to those identified above, will be of help.

6.4
Leadership Styles

A leadership style is basically the way in which a manager or team leader manages and interacts with the team and how they actively involve their team in the decision-making process. We shall now consider a continuum, which at one extreme identifies an autocratic style and at the other extreme identifies a participative style. We shall look at four particular styles in detail.

(a) Autocratic style

This particular style is the one whereby a manager or team leader makes every decision on his or her own without seeking or welcoming any input from the team whatsoever. This type of manager gives orders, often using a 'tell' style, and inevitably expects total obedience from the team. In this type of working environment, there is often a 'fear factor' accompanied by implied threats or coercion to ensure that the manager's instructions/orders are carried out. It therefore follows that managers who adopt this particular style do not expect or require any creativity or input from their team.

(b) Benevolent autocratic

In some ways this type of style is similar to that of the autocratic style, in so far as the manager will make almost every decision without involving the team. One main difference is that in adopting this style of a benevolent autocratic, the manager has at least some consideration for the team members. This type of manager still demands and expects obedience from the team at all times, although threats are not necessarily seen as the only way to achieve business results. It is more likely that team members are able to undertake their duties for their own benefit, with possibly some point of incentive or reward when they successfully do so (or alternatively some kind of threat or disincentive if they do not). However, in a similar way to the autocratic manager, the benevolent autocratic does not expect nor ask for any input or ideas from the team members.

(c) Consultative style

The consultative manager, as the name implies, consults the team before making decisions and requests ideas and suggestions from the team. Each issue that arises is dealt with in a joint way, between the manager/team leader and the team itself. A manager or team leader does, however, retain full responsibility for any decisions made, and the decision when it is made is solely that of the managers. In other words the manager has the final say.

(d) Participative style

This type of manager shares all and every decision with the team members. Without exception, the team gets together and collectively agrees on what happens next. The manager then still has responsibility for implementing the decision made, although, in effect, the manager would have played exactly the same role as each member of the team in reaching that particular decision.

Each of us tends to have one preferred managerial style which we tend to use naturally. Sometimes it is easier to revert from one style to another style depending upon the particulars of any situation being faced. Equally, some managers or team leaders cannot, in reality, switch from one style to another, although training, coaching and a desire to self-develop can help in this respect.

A summary of the main advantages and disadvantages of each of the four styles that we have discussed above now follows.

Autocratic

Main advantage
- *Can achieve success very quickly, particularly in the short-term.*

Main disadvantage
- *Will not motivate team members.*

Benevolent Autocratic

Main advantage
- *May incentivize team members through reward and recognition.*

Main disadvantage
- *Does not take advantage of initiative or ideas from team members.*

Consultative

Main advantage
- *Incorporates and welcomes ideas from the team.*

Main disadvantage
- *No concept of empowerment or decision-making authority given to the team.*

Participative

Main advantage
- *Lets everybody feel involved in the decision-making process.*

Main disadvantage
- *Due to everybody's involvement this style can be slow and cumbersome.*

6.5
Having Respect as a Team Leader

The ways in which a team leader can gain respect and credibility are obviously wide and varied. Significant influences on how this may be done depend on the culture of the organization, the functions being undertaken, the size of the team, what the team have been used to in the past, the expectations of the team in the future, the ambitions and desires of the current team leader, and so on.

We shall look at three particular ways in which respect and credibility may be earned as a team leader:

- *The personality of a team leader.*
- *Confidence in the role.*
- *The implied positional power of being a team leader.*

The personality of a team leader is always going to be very important because it is a key influence in determining the relationship a team leader has with the team, and also line management and peers. You will realize that defining the 'right' personality is almost impossible, although some of the more critical dimensions can be seen as follows.

- *Building positive relationships with the team, line management and peers.*
- *Appearing to have a confident personality (even when in fact this is not the case!).*
- *Portraying a positive attitude.*
- *Being keen to thrive in an atmosphere of open and genuine two-way communication.*
- *Creating an atmosphere in which team members' opinions and input are encouraged, respected and valued.*

In this respect, a team leader needs to be aware that having a 'too powerful' personality can smother the team and be overpowering. It can also portray a vision of appearing insincere, or possibly being overoptimistic and even naive. A team leader needs to be seen as being competent to hold that position. Some still believe that a team leader needs to have done each of the roles currently being carried out within the team, before he or she has the credibility to be the team leader. You will have your own views as to whether this is the case in your own organization, although more current views would indicate that being a manager or team leader is about achieving results through others, rather than being a subject matter expert on each and every job and role that is carried out within the team.

However, when the team leader does have a sound and expansive knowledge base, he or she should then be looking to do the following:

- *Sharing the knowledge with the team to enable enhanced team performance and individual self-development.*
- *The team leaders should make sure that they keep their own levels of knowledge current and up-to-date. One danger here is to try to convince everybody you are 'the fount of all knowledge'. This is clearly a naive approach, because nobody is 'fool proof' – team leaders and managers will make mistakes like everybody else.*
- *As a team leader you should be genuinely interested in helping your team members enhance their own levels of knowledge and to learn from you at every opportunity.*
- *Your own levels of knowledge or skills would make you an obvious candidate to become a mentor or coach for some members of your team.*

There are some potential dangers here, including team leaders trying to convince themselves and the teams that they are absolutely perfect. They then may be portrayed as the 'office know-all', as arrogant and even aloof.

We can also see that each team leader has an element of power implied as a result of that particular role, and it is there for all to see. This implies that any team leader role will give implied authority to the person who is undertaking that role. This 'position power' can be used to give direction to the team, influence the structure and activities of the team, and hopefully provide ongoing reassurance and support to every member of that team. Furthermore, this 'position power' also enables a team leader to act as a role model. In some cases, this power is open to abuse, and the team leader may become dictatorial, or take advantage of some of his or her team members or in extreme circumstances bully individuals.

The role of a team leader is always very challenging, and this becomes increasingly the case. As a leader the team will be looking to you to be positive at all times. Remember the maxim 'behaviour breeds behaviour' and the way you are will have a key influence on the way your team feel. This can be sometimes a considerable challenge, particularly if you are not feeling yourself that day, or you have had some bad news, or just completed a difficult meeting with your boss. Earlier on in this section we looked at two-ways in which you could undertake a self-review of your strengths and developmental areas as a team leader. In fact, how you perceive yourself and how your team perceives you may be quite similar or your view and their views can be quite different. Sometimes when these differences are highlighted to the team leaders concerned, they are totally surprised at how others see them.

It is an excellent exercise to begin the process of understanding how you see yourself as a team leader and how your teams see you. Below is an example of a simple questionnaire that can be completed by yourself and each of your team members. Once this is done your opinion and your team's opinions should be compared – ideally, and hopefully in your case, you would be able to have an open and frank discussion about your strengths and developmental areas as a team leader. The questionnaire below could be used merely as the beginning of an ongoing debate between you and your team – this whole exercise can be a very powerful one for you as a team leader who should be retaining an open mind about how you can learn from this, and how you can improve your skills in the future. Your team members will know that they can talk to you in an open and honest way, say what they feel and have their views respected and valued.

Ultimately, the feedback will be of value only if you as team leader are seen to act upon it. Your team members, having raised issues, will now expect you to take some sort of action to show that you have given considerable thought to what has been said.

Attribute	Always	Sometimes	Never
Positive			
Enthusiastic			
Decisive			
Sense of Humour			
Confidence			
Business Focused			
High Levels of Energy			

Figure 6.4

This is effectively an upward appraisal or upward feedback process and as a team leader there is a need to be open minded, and in no way defensive when receiving your team's thoughts. It is the easy way out to become sensitive and defensive when team members give you feedback and opinion that is less than glamorous. You really need to try to understand why your team members hold the views and opinions that they do. More often than not they have a very good reason for expressing the views that they do. It is sometimes easier if they can support their opinions by giving specific examples as illustrations.

Again, a team leader should be (must be?) seen to be receptive to the views of the team and to take the opportunity to value their opinions and to learn from them.

6.6
Delegation

Delegation is a key management skill and it is one of the main ways in which a manager or team leader can achieve objectives through the team. From the outset, we need to be very clear that delegation is not about abdication or dumping various activities on members of your team. Delegation is a very positive management skill and should be more about empowerment and motivation, which can have some positive benefits as follows:

- *Delegation helps to develop members of your team, giving them the opportunity to learn new skills and illustrate their future potential.*
- *Delegation enables the team to become more involved in the 'bigger picture' and this may be motivational in itself.*
- *When work is delegated, a relationship between delegator and delegatee is enhanced, with greater elements of trust.*

From the manager's or team leader's perspective, delegation also enables him or her to deliver more output or activity from the team overall. It enables managers to make more use of their own (and more expensive) time and should facilitate their own decision-making process.

It is not always as straightforward (whatever is!), because the delegators themselves may not be that keen to delegate. Some reasons for this situation could be:

- *The delegator may think that it is easier to do the job himself (or herself) rather than to delegate.*
- *Previous experience of delegating may endorse this view.*
- *The delegator may actually enjoy doing part of a job which in fact should be delegated ('play-penning').*
- *The delegator may prefer to keep some information back, as a form of self-protection.*
- *The delegator may feel uncomfortable delegating, because this may be perceived as showing a sign of weakness by asking somebody else to do something.*
- *The delegator may not trust the work team.*
- *The delegator may feel that by delegating he or she will be losing control of what is going on. Quite often, however, reality takes over. Quite simply delegation would have to take place because otherwise the delegator would sink without trace. He or she would have too much to do and ultimately have to rely (quite rightly) on the effective support of the team. Delegation means that the delegator (manager or team leader) is passing on responsibility for a particular task or activity to a member of the team. We need to be very clear here that the delegator is giving authority to a member of the team and on every occasion ultimate responsibility for successfully delivering whatever has been delegated remains with the delegator. Remember delegation is not abdication!*

6.7
An Overview of the Process of Delegation

Effective delegation usually follows the various steps detailed below:

(a) *The manager or team leader considering the overall skills and abilities of the team. There may need to be thought given as to what tasks, duties or functions can be delegated to which specific members of the team.*

(b) *For each piece of work that is being delegated, objectives need to be discussed and agreed between the delegator and the delegatee. Both parties must be very clear about what is being delegated and what the delegatee is expected to achieve.*

(c) *The delegation needs to be planned, and this process will begin by the delegatee being fully briefed so that he or she is clear about what will be happening in the future and how progress will be reviewed. In addition the delegator needs to be keeping track of progress and probably regular review meetings will take place. Of course, the appropriate (i.e., in reality what is available) resources need to be obtained to enable the delegatee carry out the agreed function.*

(d) *That the delegatee carries out the function without unnecessary interference. The manager or team leader needs to manage the delegatee in the ways that have been agreed and not to interfere!*

(e) *Regular monitoring – regular reviews, as we hinted at above, need to take place to make sure that progress is going to plan and that all activities will enable the agreed task or objective to be completed by the agreed time, or even ahead of schedule.*

(f) *Once completed the delegated task activity should be reviewed. Always, the delegatee benefits from having feedback on performance, and both delegator and delegatee benefit from this review process to see what could be done differently, if anything, next time.*

The types of responsibilities suitable for delegation may include:

- *Functions that the members of your team can do as well as you! Perhaps they can do them even better than you!*
- *Tasks or functions that can be used to develop members of your team – this will be motivational for them, and will also help to develop the skills base of the team, facilitate job cover for the future, and perhaps help the individual's future career aspirations.*
- *Tasks or functions that are medium or lower priority.*
- *Aspects of a manager's or team leader's role that are more routine.*
- *Any function whatsoever that should be done at a more junior level because it is more cost effective to do so.*
- *Possibly any aspects of the delegator's role that are of particular appeal to a member of the team.*

Unit 7

Motivation

7.1
What is Motivation?

Motivation can be described as:

- *A kind of drive that makes us want to do something.*
- *A way of getting somebody else to do something that we want him or her to do.*
- *A sort of spirit that comes from within ourselves.*
- *A force that can be 'stimulated' when we need to do something.*
- *Something that can be seen as an incentive.*

In the context we are considering, motivation is about the desire to do something in a positive way, and it means that somebody will do something because they want to do it. Motivation in a slightly different context could mean doing something because of fear, or because we *have* to do something.

Some of the ways in which you can motivate somebody in a positive way include:

- *Recognize in some way what they have done so far.*
- *Confirm how important this particular task is.*
- *Incentivize them in some way.*
- *Give them the confidence to do this particular activity.*

What we need to understand, therefore, is that motivation is not an exact science. For each of us as individuals motivation means slightly different things. It can be either a conscious or unconscious activity, which means that we may be actually aware or unaware of what is motivating us at any one particular point in time. Undoubtedly, motivation is a potentially very powerful force and can cause an individual to act in a particular way and sometimes in a way in which that person has not acted before.

In the workplace, for every employee there will be different motivators and de-motivators. We have already mentioned that individuals are motivated by different things; similarly they are de-motivated by different things. Nevertheless, as we will see a little later on when we consider some theories of motivation, it is possible to categorize some motivators and de-motivators in more general terms and begin to understand how we achieve, in most cases, motivational or de-motivational effects.

Some examples of motivators include:

- *Starting a new job, either by a promotion or a move to a different team or section.*
- *Receiving a financial incentive, such as a bonus or annual pay award.*
- *Receiving positive feedback from your manager or colleague for a job well done.*
- *Being part of a team that has achieved their business objectives.*
- *A personal motivation of completing something you have set out to do.*

In a similar way, examples of potential de-motivators are:

- *Possibly losing your job or part of a job.*
- *Constantly being 'put down' by your manager.*
- *Coming so close to achieving something you set out to do but not quite making it.*
- *Working as part of a team in a bad working atmosphere and involving personality clashes.*

7.2
Some Motivational Theories
Maslow's hierarchy of needs

Abraham Maslow was an American psychologist and he argued that motivation can be considered at five different levels, which can be illustrated as shown in Figure 7.1.

Overall, using Maslow's model, the psychology is that some element of social needs relates to the needs of an individual employee to have job security in an acceptable working world, a regular salary in the context of known job security, and working for an organization that has supportive personnel policies.

As an individual 'goes up' the hierarchy, he or she will see the importance of interpersonal relations increase, with colleagues and line management, for example.

Further up the hierarchy again, the importance to an individual of work itself and how an individual can be motivated by 'doing' a particular role becomes much more significant.

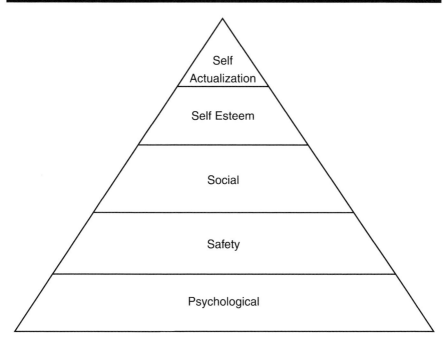

Figure 7.1

Towards the top end of the hierarchy the individual employee will be motivated by having responsibility and will actively seek responsibility in the work that he or she does. In addition, individuals will seek, expect and proactively look for recognition for the work that they do. At these stages career advancement becomes very important to an individual, as does the 'influence' they have in an organization.

Considering each level of Maslow's hierarchy in more detail:

- **Psychological needs**
This is the need for an individual to have basic needs and requirements fulfilled. Examples of such basic needs include food, shelter, and even fresh air!

- **Safety needs**
At this level, an individual looks for security and stability in the working environment. As we have mentioned above, this would apply job security, and a known and stable work environment.

- **Social needs**
This level of the hierarchy refers to an individual's need to have affection, friendship and a sense of 'belonging' or 'worth' to their particular team or business unit.

These psychological, safety, and social needs Maslow categorized as 'lower' needs, and further up the hierarchy there are two further 'higher' needs.

- **Esteem needs**

This is where an individual looks for the motivation of achieving a particular goal, and to have the opportunity to gain self respect.

- **Self actualization**

For Maslow, this was the ultimate motivational force and in the context of this model, this level would see an individual's full potential being reached.

As a guiding principal for Maslow's hierarchy, each individual would begin at the base of the hierarchy. Maslow argued that you would then progress up the hierarchy, not reaching the next stage until the previous stage had been fully satisfied. We can see that each of us could be at different stages in the hierarchy at different stages in our career, or even at different times in a month or week – we can therefore go up and down the hierarchy, depending upon the particular circumstances in the workplace at that time.

7.3
McGregor – Theory X and Theory Y

Douglas McGregor put forward a slightly different view on how individuals were motivated, and he argued that there were two main alternatives which we shall explore a little below. McGregor's views were written in the 1950s and there is a danger of immediately assuming that they are therefore too historic to be relevant today. When you look at the views that he put forward, you can draw your own conclusions as to the relevance, or otherwise, of his ideas in your own workplace (and other workplaces which you may be familiar with). For many of the major motivational theories, although they were written some time ago, for reasons which were probably unintentional at the time they have become almost 'timeless' and large parts of the theories that were written decades ago still apply without doubt in today's working world.

McGregor's guiding principles saw ways in which people could be motivated falling into two main categories, which were primarily based on how a manager was to see and value the individuals within his or her own team.

The Theory X view

This aspect of McGregors' model assumed the following:

- *That individuals have an inherent dislike for work and have long avoided it if they possibly can.*

- *That members of the workforce, if given the option, would rather be 'controlled and directed' and work in an environment where they know exactly what they need to do and how they need to do it.*
- *Building on the above point, Theory X assumes that individuals want to avoid any aspect of responsibility and do not have any ambition to pursue a career, but will develop themselves or learn.*
- *Job security is seen as primarily important.*
- *The Theory X principles also assume that as individuals dislike work they need to be incentivized to do anything and effectively threatened in some way if they then do not go on to produce or deliver.*

The Theory Y view

The Theory Y view is almost diametrically opposed to that in Theory X, and puts forward the following ideas:

- *Given the appropriate working environment, individuals can actually enjoy their work and in fact do not have an inherent dislike for work itself.*
- *Personal satisfaction in doing a particular job is very important if an individual is to be fully committed to contributing towards the achievement of business objectives.*
- *Individuals have the need to seek self-fulfillment, to organize themselves and to be 'self starters', in order to give their best and contribute to the maximum effect towards the achievement of business objectives.*
- *A Theory Y assumption is that individuals prefer not to be directed or controlled.*
- *Again, Theory Y assumes that, given the appropriate working environment, individuals are keen to learn and self-develop and actively seek responsibility.*

7.4
Frederick Herzberg
The motivation – hygiene theory

Frederick Herzberg was an American Professor of Psychology at Western Reserve University, Cleveland. He undertook some research, initially among accountants and engineers and later in many other organizations across the United States and Europe, and he concluded that individuals have two (very) different sets of needs.

Reflecting back in time, Herzberg believed that the earlier views on motivational theory had considered only the employee's working environment. Herzberg saw the importance of the working environment as being one of many key factors when considering individual motivation. He therefore began to develop a series of ideas that revolved around the experiences an individual has in the workplace itself.

Herzberg believed that work itself can be a motivator. At the time he put forward this idea it was seen as being unusual because it was new. The Theory X view, for example, was one of many that assumed that individuals had to be rewarded or incentivized to even get them to the workplace! Herzberg believed, very strongly, that a job can potentially provide a very powerful motivating force for the individual employee to achieve both personal satisfaction and growth.

Herzberg made a distinction between what he called hygiene factors and motivational factors.

Hygiene factors

Herzberg used this aspect of his theory to describe the importance of working conditions, management policies, working relationships with colleagues and salary packages. These were the 'basic needs' which were there, in Herzberg's view, to remove any underlying sources of potential dissatisfaction from the workplace, rather than to be motivators in themselves.

These 'hygiene factors' would appear to be there to maintain the 'status quo'. If they were seen to be at an acceptable level they will not, Herzberg believed, make employees work harder or do more than was required – employees would therefore be doing enough to get by rather than to be motivated to do anything extra.

Motivational factors

Herzberg saw motivational factors as being those that described individual employee's feelings of achievement, of self-development and the way in which they were recognized for a job well done, and were factors that would be available in jobs that offer sufficient challenge and the potential to develop each individual. These factors were therefore more than the hygiene factors outlined above – it was these factors that Herzberg saw as being the ones that do motivate in a positive way rather than being merely 'preventative' like the hygiene factors.

7.5
Some Ways of Making Work More Rewarding

If we were to draw on some of the more positive elements of the theories we have just considered about motivation, we would see, for example:

Individuals, as they progressed further up Maslow's hierarchy of needs, actually pursued their own needs to self-develop, to be seen to do their job well; the

Theory X view argued that individual employees actually enjoy work and will proactively seek responsibility; Herzberg saw some key motivators like seeking recognition and responsibility and striving for achievement as being important.

In this context the concept of job enrichment becomes important.

Job enrichment means that individuals in the workplace would:

- *Have more control over and responsibility for the work that they do.*
- *Work in an environment where they would be receiving ongoing feedback on what they do.*
- *Be able to pursue their own self-development in the workplace.*
- *Have the facility to achieve more responsibility.*

Jobs can actually be designed in particular ways in order for them to become 'enriched'. Some jobs naturally enable individuals to complete the whole task alone or are ones that naturally suit individuals who prefer to work on their own (and therefore have the responsibility for completing them themselves).

Job enrichment would also mean the following:

- *That a job would offer increasing levels of complexity to an individual over a period of time. This means that the job would offer the chance for individuals to develop within that job as that particular job became more complex, or demanding or challenging over time.*
- *Where the particular job is important in itself, which usually means that other members in the organization (or perhaps outside of the organization) would be depending upon that particular job being done well.*
- *Critically, new parts of a job, or tasks to be done, are genuinely seen as opportunities rather than something that is expected or demanded of an individual employee.*
- *Where individual employees seek and are able to work in an environment where they have, in fact, a degree of autonomy. This principle applies on an individual employee basis, or at a team or group level as well. These days this concept is often called 'empowerment'.*
- *Another key factor here is where individual employees are able to receive ongoing feedback and guidance as a regular part of 'business as usual'. We must be careful not to confuse job enrichment with either job rotation or job enlargement.*

  Job rotation occurs where an individual employee can be moved from one job to another at a broadly similar level. One main advantage of utilizing the principle of job rotation in the workplace is that it enables job cover to be available at times of staff shortages, perhaps, or cover for colleagues on holiday or being away from the workplace for some other reason. Job rotation can therefore give increased flexibility rather than being necessarily motivational in itself. Job rotation, does, however, enable a team of people to become more multi-skilled by being able to do a number of **different** jobs, albeit that they will be of relatively similar degrees of complexity.

Job enlargement occurs where an individual has more to do (i.e., more tasks or functions) of a similar level of challenge or complexity added to the current role. While this approach may not necessarily in itself be motivational, it can be seen to add to an individual's skill set even though the new skills being learnt are at the same level. In many of our working environments, where there are major constraints on available resources, all of us are continually being asked to take on more, and job enlargement is an example of this.

7.6
Appraisal Principles

An appraisal system has many purposes which we shall consider later in this section. One of its main functions is to enable an organization to evaluate how well its people are performing. Typically an appraisal system enables each individual to have a series of targets or objectives which need to be met, usually on an annualized basis. Some appraisal systems are for the managerial population only, although these days many more organizations are including the whole of their people resource under one simple appraisal system.

7.7
Advantages of Having an Appraisal System in Place

If you have an appraisal system in your own organization you will be familiar with some of these principles, and may even be able to add one or two of your own. Some of the main benefits of having an appraisal system in place include:

- *The appraiser has a formal opportunity to discuss the team member's job performance.*
- *It enables regular feedback to be given on an individual's job performance against performance targets or objectives.*
- *At these performance reviews, the appraisee's training needs are discussed.*
- *Each of these formal reviews is usually documented so that a permanent record can be kept, and a copy provided to the appraiser, appraisee and probably personnel.*
- *The appraisal system is not only retrospective (i.e., considering past performance) it also looks forward to the future and, particularly at the end-of-year review,*

projects forward and discusses objectives, plans and targets for the months ahead.

- *A formal appraisal review gives an opportunity for the appraiser to recognize success and highlight any areas for individual development.*
- *Appraisees, at appraisal time, also have the opportunity to formally review how they feel they have performed with their appraiser (usually their line manager).*
- *Appraisees have an opportunity to share with their appraiser their aspirations and ambitions.*

The frequency of these events varies from organization to organization. One popular approach is to have the formal annual review, and to perhaps have a mid-year review as well. More often these days, because the increasing importance of the people resource is being more widely recognized, appraisal reviews are sometimes carried out quarterly. In any case, 'best practice' would indicate that any appraisal system should be ongoing. This means that any feedback, positive or otherwise, should really be provided on an ongoing basis, that is when it actually happens. This means that at appraisal time, there really should be 'no surprises' being discussed between the appraiser and appraisee.

In the real world, having an appraisal system is not always perfect. In the section above we have considered some of the advantages of having an appraisal system in place. There are some potential major disadvantages, again some of which you may be familiar with, which are highlighted below:

- *The appraisers/line managers have not had the proper training to carry out appraisals.*
- *The appraisers/line managers may not be fully committed to the appraisal system.*
- *The appraisees may not believe their line managers are sufficiently qualified to make judgements about their job performance.*
- *The appraisees may feel that their line manager will not look at their job performance objectively, or fairly, in comparison with others.*
- *For some individuals, their job performance may be difficult to quantify, and their objectives difficult to measure.*
- *The whole issue of appraisal becomes even more sensitive if, as is often the case, appraisal is linked to pay.*
- *The appraisal system may be seen as a very time-consuming exercise which is primarily bureaucratic.*
- *Experience of previous appraisal systems may mean that managers/appraisers/ appraisees are very suspicious, even cynical, about how much 'value' the whole system will add.*

7.8
Individual Performance Objectives

Part of the appraisal process means that the appraisee is 'assessed' in terms of job performance against agreed targets or objectives. Any team leader or manager, therefore, needs to ensure that each of his or her team members has effective objectives or targets to enable them to manage to best effect through their people.

'Best practice' means that each individual's objectives or targets has the following features:

- **Specific**

Each objective or target that is set must be exact and both appraiser and appraisee should be clear about what it is that needs to be achieved.

- **Measurable**

Here an agreed form of measurement needs to be put in place which means that a target or objective must be defined in terms that are easily measurable. Examples of measurability include cost, time, and output levels.

- **Achievable**

Here we are looking for any objective or target to state what needs to be achieved during any particular part of the appraisal year.

- **Realistic**

Any objective or target that is discussed and agreed needs to be one that is demanding (in terms of 'stretching' the appraisee to perform to maximum ability) but also one that can ultimately be attainable. If any target is set unrealistically high the effect could well be demotivational from the outset.

- **Timely**

Any target or objective should contain specific time frames in which every objective or target or part of one should be achieved.

As you will already have worked out, not all objectives and targets can be set in this way. If, for example, you work on a production line or in a sales environment, it is more straightforward to agree 'SMART' objectives. Alternatively, if you work for an organization where objectives or targets are more difficult to set or quantify then having 'SMART' objectives will be more difficult. Examples of such roles could be working as a Personnel Officer, or as a Counsellor.

7.9
The Appraisal Interview

We have already noted that at the formal appraisal review there should be 'no surprises'. Nevertheless, both appraiser and appraisee need to prepare thoroughly for this formal interview.

There are three main areas for the appraiser and appraisee to consider:

(1) *For both parties to have collected factual data-based evidence which can be used to appraise performance against agreed objectives or targets.*

(2) *For both appraiser and appraisee to consider the appraisee's developmental needs, which can either build on existing strengths or focus on any areas of job performance that need to be improved.*

(3) *Both parties need to plan the appraisal interview itself.*

7.10
The Structure of the Appraisal Meeting

Your own organization will have a particular way of carrying out appraisal reviews and the way in which these reviews are carried out will vary, sometimes considerably, from organization to organization. Here are some key points for you to consider:

- *At the start of the meeting, the appraiser needs to be sure that the apprasiee is as relaxed as possible. Both appraisee and appraiser can benefit from this occasion, although for some appraisees it can be particularly nerve racking.*
- *An environment for the interview needs to be created so that the appraisee is comfortable and can fully contribute to the meeting. After all, appraisal is supposed to be a two-way process!*
- *As soon as possible, a review needs to take place of the previous year's job performance, with the main focus being on any agreed targets or objectives – due emphasis should be given to any of these targets or objectives which are agreed to be the most important.*
- *For each of the main objectives or targets, there needs to be an agreement reached between appraiser and appraisee as to what standard of performance has been achieved. If both parties have brought their own 'evidence' or data this can be quite straightforward. However, this is not always the case, because sometimes the appraiser and appraisee have very different recollections of what actually happened!*
- *Throughout the appraisal interview, the appraiser needs to ensure that there is an appropriate mixture of positive and developmental feedback and guidance.*

- *Probably a little later in the interview, the appraisee's developmental needs should be discussed (as we have mentioned earlier on).*
- *From the above point any specific training needs should be discussed and agreed, with particular emphasis on what training support can actually be provided, and is realistic to provide.*
- *Towards the end of the interview the appraiser and appraisee should agree an action plan which projects the way forward for the coming months.*
- *As appropriate a further review meeting could be arranged.*

7.11
Being an Appraiser

As discussed above, an appraisal meeting should be a two-way process and being an appraiser is a skilled role. Some of the main attributes of an effective appraiser are:

(1) Listening skills

Clearly during an appraisal interview, it is not usual to interrupt or to keep interrupting the appraisee when he or she is speaking. In the interview itself a period of silence from the appraisee may not necessarily mean that he or she does not have anything to say; more likely he or she is thinking through what has just been said or discussed and considering how to reply. Being an effective listener is quite an advanced skill and it is always dangerous to assume that you know what the appraisee is thinking about.

To facilitate your listening skills, during an appraisal interview it is often helpful to take notes in order to accurately record what has been said or agreed.

(2) Body language

During an appraisal interview the appraiser should always try to exhibit positive body language. For example, during any periods of silence do not sit there are drum your fingers!

Throughout the interview the appraiser should always try to maintain good eye contact with the appraisee. Similarly, the appraiser should always be aware of the appraisee's own body language and try to understand the messages they are conveying and establish whether what is actually being said verbally is consistent with the body language.

(3) Questioning techniques

During the interview the appraiser will ask many types of questions, often dependent upon the type of issue that is being discussed or the purpose for which they are being used. Examples of types of questions used in an appraisal interview are an open question (beginning what, why, how, where); a closed question (which usually leads to a yes or no answer and can be used to establish points of clarity); a reflective question (which can be used to check your own understanding of what the appraisee has just said).

(4) Giving feedback

Essentially throughout the appraisal interview the appraiser should give feedback to the appraisee which should be in the form of either praise or constructive criticism. In any case all the feedback given should be open, honest and appropriate. In terms of the appraisal process, feedback should enable appraisees to learn more about themselves, in terms of their own job performance and how they may improve in the future. Feedback should be data based and refer to something that actually happened. It must not refer only to bad news, or mistakes or things that have not gone to plan. Feedback is about recognizing success also and so all appraisers must not forget to tell one of the team when he or she has done a job particularly well!

Unit 8

Training

Training is a word often used quite loosely in organizations and there is still a view that says if there is a problem let us do some training and 'it will all be alright'. Well, perhaps the solution to a business performance issue may well be training, but there again it may not!

When training is made available, it is a way of helping either you or one of your team members improve job performance. It may help to develop a particular area of your own knowledge or skills and it may be something that you wish to do to facilitate your learning or preparation for a job that you want to do (hopefully) at some stage in the future.

From a business perspective training can have the following benefits:

- *It enables each member of staff to perform to optimum capacity.*
- *It can facilitate new entrants to a team or organization acclimatizing to their role more quickly.*
- *Generally, it means that jobs will be done in a more thorough, reliable and rigorous way.*
- *With a trained workforce, it is easier to facilitate job rotation during times of holiday, change or sickness.*
- *Training itself can be motivational for employees.*
- *Any 'learning organization' is probably one that is always forward looking and training helps to keep it there for the future.*

The opposite of most of these points is also training, because if an organization does not invest the time and money required to train its people, it is quite possible that:

- *Rules and regulations will not be followed.*
- *Quality of work will be unreliable.*
- *Levels of complaints may rise.*
- *Time will be used inefficiently, on an individual and collective basis.*

- *Production deadlines may be missed.*
- *Levels of product knowledge will not be what they should be.*
- *Any competitors who are undertaking the required levels of training will soon start to take your customers!*

8.1
The Training Process

In this section we shall be looking at the various (four) main stages of the training process.

(a) Identifying training needs

At this first stage it needs to be understood how well a particular team or business unit is performing. This means having a clear understanding of what level of knowledge and skills each individual team member has, and how well, in fact, these knowledge and skill levels are being applied. We then can trust the reality of what is actually happening against what we would like to see, in other words how we would look for the team to perform. By implication, we will be clarifying the differences between current levels of knowledge and skills, and the levels which we would like them to be achieving.

This difference between the reality and the ideal is known as a performance gap or 'training gap'.

Remembering what we said in the opening few lines of this section: we do, of course, need to be sure that any 'shortfalls' in an individual team member's job performance can be overcome by training.

(b) Preparing the training plan

This part of the training process builds on (a) and looks to clarify exactly what the training should be expected to achieve.

At this stage, then, the 'training objectives' need to be defined so that all involved are absolutely clear about what is happening, when and why. The team leader or manager also needs to decide who will be taking part in this particular training, and when and where the training events will take place. It also has to be decided how the training will take place, and quite often there will be an ideal and a reality. It may be that the preferred training method is not available either because of cost or timescale. Either way, bearing in mind these realities, the team leader needs to be very clear about what facilities and equipment are required, and are available in practice.

Arguably most important of all, both the team leader and each individual team member that is involved in the training needs to be absolutely clear what learning will take place during the training that is to be undertaken.

Finally, at this stage, and also crucially, the costs involved need to be estimated as accurately as possible. In today's world of (severe) budgetary constraints cost can be a prohibitive factor. Sometimes part of the training plan includes a cost/benefit analysis, which means that when the plan is proposed to senior managers, it can be clearly seen that as a result of whatever financial investment that is being made there will be a (much) greater payback to the business after the training.

Once the plan has been completed and 'signed off' by the business, then preparation to turn the plan into reality should take place.

(c) Implementation of the training plan

It is at this stage that the training plan is put into practice and, like any good plan, as team leader or manager you will need to adopt some of the best practices of effective planning. In this case it may mean amending the plan if required, although in any case the plan will need careful and regular monitoring to make sure that it is progressing as expected.

Throughout this implementation stage, you will, as team leader, be aware of the progress of each individual member of your team as he or she undergoes the training. This requires a close awareness that, in reality, each of your team members will learn at different rates, in different ways and possibly for different reasons. While you will be looking for each trainee/team member to successfully undergo the training that is available, you will need to accommodate individual variances while each individual should be looking to learn up to the maximum of his or her capabilities.

(d) Evaluation

In this fourth stage, evaluation is where you review what has happened and consider how well the whole process has gone. It may be that you would consider what could (or should) have been done differently, and evaluation is a crucial part of the learning process. In fact, some experts argue that the whole training process should be evaluated at each stage, beginning at the identification of training needs. In this way, it is argued that with each stage of the process being evaluated as you go along, there is more chance of the whole process adding maximum value to the business.

Whichever style you adopt, evaluation is crucial because it invariably provokes discussion and debate and should help your team and business consider how things could be done differently or better next time round. Examples of how this can be done include:

- *Questionnaires to be completed by the trainees, possibly at the end of the training event.*
- *Questionnaires to be filled out by the trainees' team leaders/line managers once they have returned to their business unit.*

- *'Follow-up' visits by the trainers to visit the trainees at work subsequent to the training event.*
- *A form of test, less popular these days, at the end of the training event.*

8.2
Training Needs

We have looked at, briefly, the first stage of the training process, the identification of training needs. We shall now go on to look at this crucial stage in a little more detail.

You will probably realize that training needs can be identified from either the business itself, the team, or from the individual.

At a business or organizational level, training needs are identified by considering issues such as:

- *What are the overall business aims?*
- *How well equipped are our people to meet the aims of the business?*
- *What level of knowledge and skills is there currently available from our people?*
- *What are the levels of knowledge and skills that will be required in the future?*

At a team level, training needs may be identified for a number of reasons, and we shall see that each of these reasons will incorporate change. Examples of such change that would imply a training need at team level include:

- *Someone from that team leaves.*
- *A change in company policy.*
- *New legislation.*
- *The introduction of a new method of approach to work.*

In simple terms, the equation to look at is the totality of skills/knowledge a team needs to have (remember this will be constantly changing over time) as against the skills/ knowledge the team currently has – the 'gap' between the two is what needs to be addressed. As a team leader, you will need to play your role in ensuring this 'gap' is accurately quantified, or as accurately as possible. This may involve having discussions with each of your team members, observing each team member in action, considering specifically the requirements of each team member's jobs against what they actually do or can do, and looking at any performance data that is available.

8.3
Which Training Method to Choose

The two main approaches that we shall consider here will be 'on the job' or 'off the job' training, both of which have their pros and cons.

The benefits of 'on the job' training include:

- *The trainer providing one-to-one relevant and up-to-date experience and guidance.*
- *Giving prompt and frequent feedback to the trainee.*
- *The opportunity to learn quickly.*

The disadvantages of this type of training could mean that any mistakes will be (very!) costly, the trainer's experience may not be up-to-date, the trainer may not actually like training, and of course the opportunity cost of allocating a person to do this training (when they could be doing something else).

The potential advantages of 'off the job' training include:

- *The trainee having a better opportunity to learn and focus more directly on the training taking place because he or she is away from the normal place of work.*
- *The training takes place away from the workplace, and will therefore not be interrupted.*
- *There should be more time to think, discuss and debate any learning issues.*

Some disadvantages of this approach are: cost, time away from the business unit, learning in 'theory' is very different from applying the training in the realities of the workplace, the venue may include being away from home.

Clearly, there will be some element of choice about which approach you choose and some influencing factors include: the specific needs of your trainees, what it is that is to be trained, costs, the resources available.

Furthermore, whatever approach that you choose, or is available, you will need to have some awareness of how each individual member of your team is likely to maximize the learning and benefit from the training. The way individuals learn is a very complex area, although some of the key issues which you should be aware of when considering how your team members will learn most effectively include:

- *When your team members are interested in what they are learning.*
- *When they can take part in the learning process.*
- *When your team members have the opportunity to discover knowledge and information for themselves rather than be 'spoon fed'.*
- *When they can learn at their own (individual) pace, which may be difficult in reality.*
- *When they are motivated to learn.*
- *When they can understand why they are learning.*

8.4
Other Training Options

As well as categorizing training between 'on the job' and 'off the job', there are other options available and we shall consider a few more here:

(1) Open learning courses

The main advantage here is that each individual trainee can work at his or her own pace and have an influence as to when the learning takes place. The training and learning itself can be taken on in smaller stages, and this will mean less time away from the workplace.

The main disadvantages of this approach include that the learner can be easily interrupted, group discussions are less likely to be involved, and this approach is almost totally reliant upon the individual trainee's self-discipline and self-motivation.

(2) Secondments

This occurs where an individual team member is placed in a different team for an agreed period of time and as such should be able to benefit from personal guidance from colleagues from elsewhere in the business. Here an individual trainee can gain experience of working in a different part of the organization and have the opportunity to try out new skills.

Disadvantages of this approach include that the person on secondment may well be seen by the 'host section' as a nuisance or hindrance, and it also assumes that the coaching support is available for the trainee.

(3) Use of rule books/guidelines/manuals

The benefit of this approach is that this reference material can be used by the trainee at the workplace and that consistent and hopefully up-dated information is available to all who use it. With luck the manuals and rule books in your organization are easy to use and to find your way around (or maybe not!).

Obviously one main disadvantage of this approach is that rule books or guidelines cannot answer questions and in fact may not contain the information that is sought.

(4) IT training

This type of training can usually be done in the trainee's own workplace, and at the individual trainee's own place. An added advantage is that the trainee is usually able to ask colleagues for support while completing the training.

As with open learning courses, the trainee can be easily interrupted and also the IT course may become out of date.

(5) Coaching

Some benefits of coaching include:

- *Consolidation of knowledge required by a trainee.*
- *Helping to translate any (theoretical) training into 'the real world'.*
- *Reinforcing the benefits of training to other team members.*
- *Reinforcing any training that has been learnt on a course as a follow-up exercise.*
- *It can be done in the workplace and therefore focuses on work and tasks that actually need to be done.*

Coaching, then, needs to be linked to an individual's development needs, possibly highlighted by a performance appraisal. For the coach to work effectively with the team member, these developmental needs should be identified in a working environment of openness, honesty and trust. Coaching is also a very visible means of providing support to the trainee in a very specific, and hopefully meaningful way.

Some of the key aspects of providing effective coaching undoubtedly include:

- *Establishing a positive relationship between the coach and the trainee.*
- *Enabling the trainee to improve job performance.*
- *Being flexible insofar as during the coaching process, new areas to focus upon may be identified.*
- *The coach must be positive throughout the coaching process without being in any way judgemental or damning.*
- *The coach needs to be approachable throughout. Undoubtedly the coaching process needs to be one that is planned, consistent and well thought out, with a mutually agreed approach discussed and agreed by the coach and the trainee.*

When making the decision for either you or one of your team members to act as a coach, I would imagine that an element of prioritization needs to take place. A decision needs to be taken as to where coaching is appropriate and will add maximum value to the business. In any case any coaching undertaken needs to be quantified in terms of specific business results and both the coach and trainee need to have a clear understanding of what they are looking to achieve. As we have already mentioned above, the coach should be a member of the team who is respected, has the required level of knowledge and interpersonal skills, and also has the capacity to take on this increased (probably time-consuming) responsibility.

Throughout the coaching process, regular reviews need to take place to ensure that both coach and trainee are comfortable that all is going to plan. Throughout the coach must project a personal and genuine interest in the trainee's efforts and give constructive and non-judgemental feedback.

Ideally, the whole coaching exercise can be beneficial to both the coach and the trainee because both parties should gain personal development from it.

Unit 9

Working in a Team

The vast majority of activities in the workplace are carried out through teamwork. Most of us are involved in a team, or several teams, probably both inside and outside of the workplace.

We need to be very clear at the outset about the distinguishing features between a team and a group.

Some of the main characteristics of a group are likely to be:

- *An environment where more formal communication takes place.*
- *Where individual team members do not expect to receive support from their colleagues within the group.*
- *Each group member is less likely to know what their colleagues are up to, and how they contribute to the overall success (or otherwise!) of the group.*
- *With the emphasis on a more formal communication approach, this may lead to any disagreements within the group becoming confrontational, or avoided or perhaps suppressed.*
- *The goals of a group are more usually imposed rather than debated and subsequently agreed by consensus.*
- *Furthermore, individual group members may not even know what the overall group objectives are.*

Some likely characteristics of a team are as follows:

- *The communication structure can be both formal and informal and it is more often the case that individuals feel more free and able to say what they feel and think.*
- *Within a team there is usually much more interdependence between individuals – a working environment where individual team members help each other and provide mutual support is encouraged.*

- *In a team, everybody should be aware of their individual objectives and how they contribute to the overall team objectives.*
- *There is a tendency towards an environment of two-way, open and honest feedback.*
- *Building on the point above, it is then more likely that all team members will feel 'empowered', involved and consulted about what the team is involved in, how they are progressing and as a result could well feel more motivated about what they are doing.*
- *In a team environment, there is wide acceptance that any tendency towards a 'blame culture' should be avoided as an absolute priority. Quite the opposite, in fact, is encouraged where individual ideas, suggestions and contributions are welcomed, recognized and incentivized.*

9.1
Distinguishing Features of Teams

There are many factors that influence the way each particular team works and operates. We shall consider some of these below.

(a) The type of organization

This is clearly an important factor because the type of organization within which the team operates will determine the team's objectives, how the team strives to achieve those objectives, the way in which the team deals with customers both internal and external, and how the individuals within that team are managed. If we were to compare two teams of clerical support workers, one being based in a Government Department and the other in a Doctor's Practice, and to investigate how they worked, using the criteria above, I suspect we would find some significant differences.

(b) The organizational culture

This is another important feature. Culture is a very complex area and is a feature of an organization that will have evolved over time and in a way that is largely dependent upon the history of the organization, the way in which it is managed and the type of work being done, for example. Sometimes culture is difficult to quantify although it is often talked about in a far too simplistic manner. It has been defined as 'the way we do things around here' (Whyte & Plenderleith – *Management*).

(c) The type of work being done

There are many possibilities here, some examples including physical work, office work, paper-based work, research, clerical duties, creative activities – the list is endless and I am sure that you can think of several other categories.

(d) The size of the team
Again there are many options here, and some would say the 'optimum' size for an effective team is between 8 and 12 members. In reality teams can be very small, sometimes even 2 or 3 members, or at the other extreme being say 20 to 30 people. There are some clear differences, some of which are immediately obvious. One example is that the smaller team would be working, inevitably, much closer together and therefore the need to get on and cooperate in what could be a quite suffocating work environment would be essential. Within this smaller team, however, communication and organization should be easier. The larger the team, the more complex the dynamics of organization become. Communication issues can become more challenging, building the team more involved, and if the group is too large it may become divided (either by necessity or by a split) into smaller groups.

(e) The team history
Really this refers to what the team has done in the past. A team with a successful track record will look to the future with confidence and may well have a team that has bonded particularly well together, where working relationships are positive, no doubt having been helped by sharing the successes of previous times. This type of team will look forward to the future with confidence, accept change as a challenge and look forward to being presented with new targets or challenges as opportunities. If a team is more recently formed they will not have such a history to look back on and the working relationships between team members will be less well developed. It takes time for relationships to become established, elements of trust to be confirmed, and for a team to gain confidence in their ability to succeed together.

(f) The importance of technology
Technology affects most of our day-to-day working lives to some extent. Some teams spend their whole working life working with technology, perhaps based at a screen or carrying out their day-to-day activities in an automated or semi-automated environment. Generally, technology enables work to be done more quickly, probably more cheaply and also ultimately with less input from the team members themselves. In addition, for those teams that spend their day working individually with technology, the dimensions of team interruptions and relationship building would work very differently from say, a team of trainers. These trainers would inevitably, by the nature of the work that they do, seek to meet regularly to discuss any courses they may be running, to generate new ideas for future training sessions or ideas around training delivery. You should be able to think of some comparisons of your own as well.

We can therefore begin to draw out some generic benefits that individuals gain from being in a work team. These include: companionship; receiving support from their colleagues; feeling part of a team; having a sense of purpose by knowing how it is their own job contributes to the overall success of the team; feeling part of something; being able to seek and receive assistance when required.

We also need to understand that the team needs: clear accountabilities and objectives, to know what it is that needs to be done to achieve success; to receive support and encouragement from the team leader or manager; for adequate (as is realistic in each particular case) resources to be made available; to be led well by their manager or team leader; to work in a stable environment, in terms of team members (in reality this may be harder to achieve).

Over time, all teams develop their own 'norms'. These 'norms' are a team's unwritten rules about how team members are expected to behave and conduct themselves while at work. Examples of such 'norms' include: dress code; attitude towards flexibility with their work; approach to their working environment, e.g., tidiness.

9.2
Roles Within a Team

There have been many ideas put forward on the various roles that are played within a team environment and one of the more widely used and respected models is that proposed by Meredith Belbin.

Belbin produced a model which he believed outlined the various roles that were necessary to be fulfilled within a team in order that that team may perform to its optimum capacity. Most individuals naturally try to obtain their preferred role within a team, and their own make-up or job strengths or personal preferences make each individual have a tendency (sometimes very strong) towards a particular role. In reality, it may not be possible for each member of a team to obtain his or her preferred role. This could lead to examples of conflict within a team whereby two or even three team members are vying with each other for one particular role. It can sometimes be the case where an individual cannot obtain a preferred role, he or she is actually adaptable enough to take on a different role, sometimes called their secondary role. In extreme cases, where an individual cannot find a role that is suitable, he or she may become de-motivated, negative and be a devisive influence within the team. That person may have to leave that particular team.

The nine roles that Belbin identified are as follows:

- **Chairman**
Usually an individual with an objective viewpoint having a leading role in achieving the team's objectives.

- **Shaper**

This person is a (or the) key influencer. Often a shaper is extrovert in nature, impatient for success and for quick progress to be achieved.

- **Plant**

Typically an intelligent person, who is naturally creative and looking to provide different alternatives of how to proceed towards the successful achievement of group objectives. The plant does not like being involved in detail and would not view lines of authority or chains of command as inhibitors to progress.

- **Resource investigator**

This person likes a challenge and is very enthusiastic and has an enquiring mind. The resource investigator likes challenges and new challenges very frequently because he or she can sometimes become bored very quickly.

- **Monitor evaluator**

This individual continually reviews the progress of the team as it evolves towards achieving its business objectives. This person is very reliable and looks for regular reviews of progress against targets throughout progress towards any objectives.

- **Completer/finisher**

An orderly individual who always likes to see things through to the end. This person does not always like change and usually prefers working in a more stable environment.

- **Team worker**

A more social member of the team who looks to promote team spirit and focuses on the social aspects of team activity.

- **Company Worker**

This individual is hard working, very organized and structured in his or her work, and in a similar way to the completer/finisher likes to work in a regular and stable environment.

- **Specialist**

An individual who may well be seconded to a team for specialist knowledge or input that he or she can provide, perhaps for a shorter period of time.

For those of you who work in teams, it is a very interesting exercise to consider who is taking or could take each role within Belbin's model. If there are any areas of duplication you may then consider what you could do about it. Either way you may have a clearer understanding of why it is each individual member of your team is performing in a particular way.

9.3
How a Team Evolves

Most would say that teams, like individuals, have a predictable in terms of stages (although not necessarily timescale) life cycle. It therefore follows that if a manager or team leader can understand where the team is in terms of this life cycle, management styles or leadership styles or behaviours can be adapted as required.

One way of quantifying the various stages in this life cycle is by using Tuckman's model. We shall now look at each stage in turn.

- **Forming**

At this first stage a group of individuals who are to form a team meet. This could actually be the first time that this group of people have met each other, although some may know each other from previous roles, and others may be complete strangers to each other. We need to assume that this team is essentially still a group of individuals. The early interactions between individuals tend to focus on relationship building and for team members to try and 'jockey' for their preferred roles or positions (as, for example, identified by Belbin) and to probably stamp their identity on the group. At this stage, the team leader always tries to retain a focus upon the actual team tasks or objectives which need to be achieved as the ultimate priority.

- **Storming**

At this stage the team members try to achieve their preferred role. There may be some interpersonal conflict which needs to be managed by the team leader. The team leader should be focusing on the issues to be managed, rather than on any individual personalities or personality clashes that surface. We also need to realize that each individual within the team will cope with this storming stage in a different way. Some may be very comfortable during this potentially unsettling phase of group development, especially if they have secured the role to which they have aspired. Alternatively some other team members may be feeling very uncomfortable either because they have not faced this situation before, or possibly because they are faced with doing a role within a team that is entirely new to them. Some individuals may not yet have established any relationships, social, work or otherwise. The team leader needs to keep fully abreast of all these developments and manage them sensitively and carefully.

- **Norming**

The group then develops to a stage of regular work activities which will be symbolized by an established decision-making process where decisions are often reached after discussion. Communications tend to be more open and working relationships continue to develop. The team leader should therefore be building a foundation for future success at this stage and be clearly aware of any areas for concern or potential concern and addressing them as soon as possible in the most appropriate way. Also, the team leader needs to ensure that each of the individual team members is feeling as comfortable as possible within the roles that he or she is asked to fulfil.

- **Performing**
According to Tuckman, at this fourth stage of the model the group will perform at its optimum level. Quite obviously the team leader seeks to maintain this level of maximum performance for as long as possible.

- **Mourning**
This is where the period of peak performance has passed, and when this actually happens depends upon many different factors. For example, the group objectives or targets being achieved, the culture within which the team operates, the management or leadership style of the team leader, the energy levels generated by the team, and the period of time involved (and that has evolved).

Other main features of Tuckman's model are:

- *If a new team member joins or an existing team leader leaves, the group as a whole will go back to the forming stage.*
- *The time period taken for a team to evolve from the forming to the performing stage depends on the particulars of each case. This may lead to a conflict of objectives between the team leader who would like to see the team evolve to the performing stage, and his or her own manager who would expect optimum performance from day one!*

9.4
Personal Development
Your own self-development

All of us from time to time will have looked to the future, in terms of our career, and to try to consider the opportunities we have. These opportunities may be in terms of developing our current role, trying to clarify what roles may be (realistically) available to us in the future and any (again realistic) timescales for when we may plan these possible changes.

The prevailing job market conditions are very tough and are likely to become even tougher. This means that all of us need to be very realistic about our future career and what we personally can do to influence that future. Each of us needs to be very clear about what our motivators are, and what is important to us personally. It therefore follows that any decision that we make regarding our future must be ours alone and done for reasons which are ultimately the best for us. It also logically follows that the primary responsibility for our self-development rests with us, personally, too.

When you are trying to achieve some sense of priority in what you are looking to do in the future then I am sure you will be debating some of the following issues:

- *How important your career is to you.*
- *Your like (or dislike) of accepting new challenges.*
- *The importance of money to you.*
- *The importance you place on your family or outside activities.*
- *How important you see your own self-development.*
- *What your ideal balance is between work and domestic activities.*

Clearly the priorities you have may well change over time, and I am sure if you look back over recent years (for those of you that have been in work long enough!) some of those issues mentioned above would have been more or less important at that time.

9.5
Being Honest

So when we look to the future, or review where we are, we need to be able to be entirely honest with ourselves, as well as being realistic about what is happening in the world around us. One way of doing this is to conduct your own 'self-review' which involves:

- *Your own self-assessment of your personal key strengths and areas that you need to develop – it is best to base this part of your assessment on what is factual rather than perceived.*
- *Your could look at your current accountabilities and role objectives and consider how well you are able to deliver these, what you excel in, and what you may find more challenging.*
- *Some regular feedback should be available from your line manager in the form of appraisals or performance reviews. Perhaps you could seek more detail and supplement this feedback with that from your peers, team members, family and friends.*
- *You could also look to endorse (or question) your present self-review with any recent historical data or records you may have in the form of appraisals or reports.*

In many ways it is a good idea to conduct a self-appraisal like this regularly, perhaps biannually, or at a frequency that is appropriate for you. In any case this process should help you to get a clearer and more honest picture of what you could be looking to do in the future and also what areas you could look to try to develop.

9.6
Changes in the Job Market

The job market has changed dramatically over recent decades as technology continues to have more and more influence. In the future the following trends will affect labour markets around the globe:

- *More and more individuals will become self-employed.*
- *'Home working' will become more popular.*
- *As we know, the 'cradle to the grave' employment 'contract' has long gone, and more and more people will be employed on short-term (probably renewable) contracts.*
- *More people will be working on a part-time basis.*
- *The world job market will continue to become 'smaller', which means that individuals will have access to job markets on a cross-border basis.*
- *Throughout all of these changes it will still remain that each of us is personally responsible for our own self-development to ensure that we remain as marketable as possible in order that we can help to fulfil our individual potential.*

9.7
Your Own Personal Development

An area that you personally need to develop or to become more adept at, or reasons for development, will be one of the following:

- *An area of technical ability that you need to improve upon.*
- *To develop a particular key competency.*
- *To improve your knowledge levels in a certain area of your job.*
- *To change the way of your current behaviour.*
- *To learn a new skill.*

These developmental areas can either be used to facilitate development in a current role, or to help to prepare for a future role or changes in your existing role. Clearly, you will be unable to look to the future in this way unless you have a solid foundation upon which to build, and at the very least have a full awareness and understanding of what it is you should be currently doing in your own role. It would also be helpful to have some knowledge about what is likely to happen in the future either in terms of your own job or any future jobs that you may aspire to. You should also be considering what support and resources you may have available to put into effect your plans for personal development.

9.8
Managerial Support for Personal Development

Either you as a team leader to members of your team, or your line manager to you, has a key role to play in supporting personal development. We have already realized that the responsibility for self-development or personal development is ours and ultimately no one else's. Nevertheless line management do have a responsibility to facilitate the kind of culture or working environment where this self-development is encouraged. Line management therefore need to be approachable for guidance, ideas and support. Other important roles line management may take in this context include:

- *Giving feedback as to how realistic plans for self-development are.*
- *Providing motivation.*
- *Acting as a coach.*
- *Creating the right environment to facilitate self-development.*
- *Leading by example by being visible.*
- *Encourage team members to be creative and innovative.*
- *Helping to develop members of the team by delegating, empowering, and involving them in decisions that affect them.*

9.9
A Personal Development Plan

This plan is exactly as the name says, personal to you. It will not be nearly as effective if this plan is 'imposed' from anywhere else – this plan has to have your ownership, endorsement and commitment because only in this way will it have the maximum chance to become reality. This plan effectively converts your own thoughts and ideas about how you can develop in your current role or prepare for a future role into reality because you have gone through the (academic) exercise of formalizing all of this. Effectively you are committing your plan to paper and enabling yourself to keep a record which can be regularly reviewed. This therefore facilitates your being able to look back over time to see where you have improved and how much progress you have made. This plan may cover a period of time that is appropriate

Individual	(Agreed) Course of Action	Target Date to be Completed	Comments Review Date	Development Needs
(1)				
(2)				
(3)				
(4)				

Figure 9.1

to your own particular needs. It may be for a number of weeks, months or even a year – in any case, like any other plan, it must be constantly reviewed, up-dated and amended in accordance with any changes that may take place.

Ideally, as we have hinted at in the previous section, line management support would be very beneficial. A regular (say monthly, for example) review with your line manager would be invaluable because you could review progress and receive some hopefully meaningful feedback from your boss.

An example of what a personal development plan could look like is illustrated in Figure 9.1.

Examples of courses of action that could be included on your personal development plan are: a secondment to a different team or business unit; perhaps being involved in a project or a particular part of your line manager's role, or the work of a colleague; attending an internal or external training course; attending a college course; undertaking some research or wider reading.

In your personal development plan I also feel it is sensible not to unrealistically over-commit yourself. It seems that if we try to focus on a maximum of three or four areas at any one time, perhaps even fewer than this, we have a greater chance of retaining the enthusiasm and desire to succeed.

Unit 10

Personal Development

When we are looking at the way we use our time, if **all** of us are honest I have no doubt that we could use the minutes in our day more effectively. We all know that time is irrecoverable, once it has passed we cannot get it back and for many of us we may argue that we are too busy to stop and review how we spend our time in any case! Ineffectively using our work and domestic time can therefore become a self-fulfilling prophecy.

To begin with it can be quite helpful to consider what we see as our own priorities, and what in fact they are now, are likely to be over, say the next 12 months and perhaps even further ahead. By thinking through what our priorities are, in terms of domestic, career, relationship, and other areas, we can then begin to see in broader terms how we should be proportionately allocating and prioritizing our time. In any one of these dimensions circumstances can change, and as a result priorities change also – this means your broader priorities and life objectives need to be regularly reviewed. Once you have done this exercise we can begin to think about how we manage our time in more detail.

Perception is everything and all of us would say we are 'busy'. It is when we actually start to define what busy is we start to come up with some interesting answers. Time is finite, and it is therefore critical that we look at how we use our time in as scientific a way as possible. We also need to be honest and ruthless in the way we carry out this analysis, although the process that we can adopt is quite simple.

One suggested way you may wish to consider for analysing your working week is as follows:

- *Make a note of everything you do in a particular day, although realistically record activities that take, say, more than 10 minutes.*
- **Accurately** *and* **rigourously** *make a note of all the things that take up your time unnecessarily (i.e., 'time stealers').*

- *Make sure that when you are recording these details you continue to do so in a way that incorporates any peaks and troughs in your work activities. This may mean that a day may be sufficient, or perhaps a week or even a month may be necessary for you to record enough information to be meaningful.*
- *Begin to categorize the amount of time you spend doing your priority activities (you should know what these priority activities are!).*

It should be very clear that you need to focus on what actually happens rather than what you wish would be happening, or what should be happening. Furthermore I also feel very strongly that it is sensible to keep a written record of all of these findings and you may find the simple grid shown in Figure 10.1 helpful in this respect.

Obviously the 9.00–5.00 span given on the chart is merely for illustrative purposes. In today's economy you may be one of thousands who work other than these hours and clearly you can amend the chart to suit your own specific circumstances.

If you wanted to, you could also conduct a similar review of how you spend your outside work activities. If you were to do this, you can then look at your work activities and how much time you actually spend doing your job priorities (you may find some interesting facts here!). Similarly, you can look on a more scientific basis about how you spend your outside work time, and again based on your 'life objectives' you may find you wish to make some (significant) amendments in how you allocate your waking hours.

Inevitably, you will find areas both in work terms and in your outside life where you should be using your time more effectively. There are always courses of action you can take, and in work you can discuss your findings with your line manager and at home discuss your findings, as appropriate, with your family.

Some ideas of How to improve your own time management

What follows is a list of ideas that you may find useful. I have no doubt you will also have some ideas of your own, which is excellent because it shows that already you are thinking about how you can improve your own use of time.

- *Make sure that you know what your job priorities are. Agree what your priorities are with your line manager, and within these priorities make sure which is first, second, and so on.*
- *Use a 'to do list', which you may find is already widely used in your own organization. In simple terms this means that every day you make a list of things that you must do, and then rank them in order of priority. Effectively you then have a check list to 'tick off' these activities as you complete them during your working day. You must clearly be aware of what is urgent and what needs to be done first, and what in fact can wait until later on.*

Day	Time	Details of Activity/Time Stealers/Events/Interruptions
Monday	9.00 am	
	10.00 am	
	11.00 am	
	12.00 pm	
	1.00 pm	
	2.00 pm	
	3.00 pm	
	4.00 pm	
	5.00 pm	
Tuesday	9.00 am	
	10.00 am	
	11.00 am	
	12.00 pm	
	1.00 pm	
	2.00 pm	
	3.00 pm	
	4.00 pm	
	5.00 pm	
Wednesday	9.00 am	
	10.00 am	
	11.00 am	
	12.00 pm	
	1.00 pm	
	2.00 pm	
	3.00 pm	
	4.00 pm	
	5.00 pm	
Thursday	9.00 am	
	10.00 am	
	11.00 am	
	12.00 pm	
	1.00 pm	
	2.00 pm	
	3.00 pm	
	4.00 pm	
	5.00 pm	
Friday	9.00 am	
	10.00 am	
	11.00 am	
	12.00 pm	
	1.00 pm	
	2.00 pm	
	3.00 pm	
	4.00 pm	
	5.00 pm	

Figure 10.1

- Be careful with your use of the telephone – this can be a major 'time stealer'. It is sometimes an idea to try to allocate time during the day to make all of your calls one after the other, if this is realistic. In any case you should prepare before making the call so that you can make any telephone conversation as concise – but always as polite – as possible.

- Attend meetings if it is right for you to do so. Ensure that any meetings you attend actually give you some 'value', or consider whether somebody else could go on your behalf, or even question the need for the meeting in the first place!

- Our best friend is paper, glorious paper! Many of us often have that sinking feeling as paper hits our desk from all directions. Your guiding principle must be 'handle each piece of paper only once'. Paper shuffling takes time, wastes time, and you may well have heard of the famous 'four D's':
  - Do it (now!)
  - Delegate it
  - Diarize it
  - Dump it (get rid of it now!)

- Concentrate on 'getting it right first time'. Perhaps in your organization, like many others, you will have heard it said that there is never time to do everything. In that same organization there is always time to make corrections or rectify errors . . . Strange concept, that one!

- Always be clear about what you are doing and why. Seek clarity when necessary to be absolutely sure that you are focusing your time on the priorities that need to be achieved.

- Be efficient with your admin and consider using an 'in tray' and 'out tray'.

- Make use of any training support that may be available to help you. Perhaps there is a training course you could attend on time management.

- Delegate when (and if!) you can.

- Avoid being caught in the 'beck and call' activity trap. You will be seen as kind, approachable, a good person to have in the team, for all of those reasons, and because people will quite happily come and off-load some of their own activities on your desk!

- Make sure that you keep focused on your own roles, responsibilities and priorities. Remember any assumptions we make about how we think we use our time will inevitably be misleading to some extent!

10.1
Counselling Skills

All team leaders or managers have, at some stage, a 'welfare role' to perform for the team. Examples of whether this type of approach may be appropriate are with an individual team member having a problem – sickness, absence from the office, performing below expectations, clash of personalities, and so on. When involved in this type of issue, the team leader is trying to be supportive and helping the team members to work through their own problems.

Essentially, the team leader is looking together with the team members themselves, to work out what the problem is. Furthermore, the team leader must try to help the team member solve the problem for himself or herself – there may even be occasions when the team leader should be guided to seek expert help or assistance. These would be occasions when the team leader clearly does not have the appropriate skills or qualifications to help on a particular occasion.

A 'counselling' approach is one whereby, in simple terms, the team leader adopts a problem-solving role. The steps outlined below show some of the key stages in this approach:

- *The problem needs to be identified. In the majority of cases this means that a team leader needs to adopt a 'non-directive' approach. This approach means using 'open-ended' questions that encourage the team member to offer some sort of explanation.*

- *Throughout this scenario, the team leader must be exercising effective listening skills, and should not be offering advice at this early stage. The primary objective is to gain an understanding about what the issue is for the team leader, and there are occasions when this may be particularly sensitive for the team leader himself or herself.*

- *During the 'counselling section' the team member may discuss something that is particularly sensitive, there may be times when there are (long) silences. This may mean that either the team member needs some more encouragement to offer some sort of explanation, or maybe he or she is using this time to think through a particular issue or to consider how to express the problems currently being faced.*

- *It will be crucial, particularly for the team member, to be able to define the issues or the problem during this stage.*

- *The team leader should also be looking to try to understand how the team member actually feels about the problems. Again similar skills are required by the team leader, as, ideally, part of this counselling process is for the team member to consider (possibly for the first time) and then hopefully verbalize, how he or she feels. This in itself should help the team member to recognize his or her own part in this problem.*

- *Depending on what the actual issue is that the team leader faces, some solutions may be fairly straightforward. For example, changes could be made in a team member's job, perhaps some of the other team members could become involved to provide support or assistance.*

- In every situation any solution that is proposed will work only if the team leader concerned firstly believes that there is a problem to be faced, and secondly then believes in any solution that is proposed. We have already seen above that ideally team members should be identifying and defining the problem they face for themselves. Similarly, they will most likely genuinely believe in the solution only if they have already put it forward themselves. This, therefore, should be encouraged during the counselling session itself, and the team member should be given the opportunity to evaluate any solutions proposed in a thorough and reflective way.
- In extreme circumstances (for example, drug addiction, relationship problems), expert/professional assistance may well be appropriate. Here, the team leader can offer further assistance by giving time off as required for the team member, obviously respecting confidences, possibly going with the team member on the first visit to see a specialist of some sort. Clearly, however, in extreme circumstances like this, in the vast majority of cases the team leader is neither qualified nor skilled to give advice or support.

In brief conclusion, counselling is one way in which a team leader can offer a supportive role to the team members when necessary. Being an effective counsellor is a skill, and these days training support is available to help team leaders to become more aware of what needs to be done. As importantly, a team leader will be sought out for support of this kind only when the team members feel they can approach the leader in the first place. Quite obviously, then, working relationships between the team leader and team members need to be ones of openness, honesty and trust.

10.2
Succession Planning

Succession planning looks into the future and projects forward all the main requirements that an organization might have in terms of its people. Succession planning should anticipate any changes that are likely to occur and what this will mean in terms of people requirements, the management that will be needed and the qualifications or training that would be required. A succession plan also incorporates the implications of any structural changes that are known, perhaps through a merger, a restructure, an amalgamation of departments or business units, for example.

Clearly, for a succession plan to work, up-to-date records of each member of staff have to be available – details like an individual's age, qualifications, experience, future job preferences and potential.

In a succession plan there are usually three main time periods that are considered:

- **Immediate term**
This would be a plan for the short-term only.

- **Medium-term**

Usually for a period of one to five years into the future.

- **Longer-term**

More difficult to quantify, and covering a period of five-ten years into the future.

In an immediate-term succession plan, the reality is that any successors in a succession plan will be those who would be immediately available, and therefore probably from within the organization (although this is not always the case). Possibly an immediate successor may be one who is already 'covering' for the line manager, or in a particular role elsewhere and will merely be confirmed in that role.

In a medium-term succession plan an organization would have more options, because they would have the scope to look both inside and outside of the organization for any successors in a particular role.

Looking at a longer-term succession plan scenario means that not all the changes that organization may face will be known. This means any planning could be done on a 'what if' basis or look to the future in a number of ways, and considering various options or scenarios. Some longer-term aspects will be a little clearer, an example of this would be those who are projected to move through an organization fairly quickly over a number of years. Such examples would include members of staff on a management development scheme. In a longer-term succession plan, an organization should also be taking the opportunity to look at the broader requirements that the organization has, or may have, of its people over a longer period of time.

Succession planning is one way of moving individuals around in an organization, possibly for promotion or transfer. It also enables an organization to cater for staff turnover, for those who exit the organization for whatever reason (for example, retirement, leaving to join another organization). In whatever circumstances, a succession plan should enable any successors in a role to have their training and development requirements both defined, planned and catered for.

Although essentially the succession plan is that – a plan – it involves people. As such, it should not be just be seen as a computer print-out but 'tells' its people what is happening. In the majority of cases, those individuals concerned need to have some sort of ownership, commitment, or 'buy in' to the process, and in particular what it means to them. A crucial part in a succession plan is managing an individual's expectations, particularly of those who had expected it to be developing their career in a particular way, but in today's world of ever-changing circumstances their own plans may need to be amended. In extreme cases some people may be so disappointed or disillusioned with their role in a succession plan that they may exit the organization.

There is no perfect solution for an organization to work to in terms of how much of a succession plan enters the public domain and how much of it should remain confidential. Key influences here are the existing practices within the organization and the expectations of the people themselves. There are some examples of organizations where succession planning is such a secret exercise that those individuals concerned are not be advised of their involvement until immediately before their new role is to commence.

10.3
Selection Recruitment and Induction

One main element of a recruitment process is for it to be professional and leaving all of those who are involved with a positive impression of the organization. An organization's recruitment process will have a reputation in the job marketplace, either positive or otherwise. Organizations are looking to attract the better people to work with them, and an effective recruitment selection process is one way of doing this. Furthermore, once people are recruited, organizations will look for staff to stay with them, rather than looking for their second job before they have settled in to their first one!

10.4
Critical Aspects of a Successful Recruitment and Selection Policy

- *All aspects of an organization's recruitment and selection policy should be known and clearly communicated to all employees.*
- *Equal opportunities policy should be fully endorsed and implemented.*
- *All recruitment and selection procedures should be seen to be fair and consistent.*
- *All those members of staff who are involved in the selection and recruitment activities should be properly selected themselves, and adequately (professionally) trained.*
- *Job advertisements, whether internal or external, must be realistic.*
- *Any person, whether already in the organization or joining the organization, must be effectively communicated to as the selection and recruitment policy proceeds. For example, an application for employment or for a particular job should always be acknowledged.*

10.5
The Key Steps in the Recruitment Process

(1) Job specification

This is where the requirements and purpose of any job are defined. Some of the criteria used to achieve this definition include: the skills and abilities necessary to do the job; the experience that would be necessary to do the job; what training would be required to help the successful candidate 'get up to speed'; any personal qualities that may be required.

(2) Application form

Any application form must be suitable for the job which is being applied for and any part of the form that is required to be filled out must be appropriate to that particular role.

In any application form it should be clearly stated what happens in terms of taking references, and specifically at what stage in the recruitment process references will be sought.

All application forms received by an organization should be acknowledged and must be treated as strictly confidential. Any recruitment information that is held on computer must be advised to all applicants as per the requirements of the Data Protection Act 1984.

(3) Advertising

Any job advertisement must be clear and able to be easily understood by all candidates or potential candidates. Advertising for a job can be a very expensive process and an organization will be looking to seek a number of candidates for the role from an advertisement first time round.

The type of detail in a job advertisement should include the following:

- *The specific requirements of the job.*
- *Any qualifications, skills and experience that would be required.*
- *A brief overview of the recruiting organization.*
- *Where the job is located.*
- *An outline of the rewards package.*
- *Details of any relocation package.*
- *Whether the job is full-time, part-time, on a contract basis, or permanent.*
- *How the first stages of the application process will work.*

(4) Selection process

There are many ways in which this selection process can take place, depending on a number of issues including cost, organizational policy, and the type of job being recruited for.

Some examples of selection procedures used today include: interviews; assessment centres; psychometric tests.

Some selection procedures include a combination of more than one of these, although whichever method or combination of methods is used, it has to be ensured that each applicant is treated in the same (fair) way.

In this context, you will need to be aware of the implications of the Sex Discrimination Act 1975, the Race Relations Act 1976 and of Equal Opportunities, Ageism and Disability legislation.

(5) Interview stage

From all the various selection procedures that are available, the interview remains the most widely used. Obviously, interviews need to be structured in a consistent and relevant way to ensure that each applicant is treated similarly.

Important issues to consider at this stage include:

- *All interviewers should be fully trained.*
- *Every interview carried out should be done so on a professional basis.*
- *Every interviewee should have the chance to ask any questions he or she may have.*
- *During the interview, probably towards the end, the interviewee should have a full understanding about what happens next.*

(6) Using references

The two types of reference most often used are those that comment on a candidate's ability and achievements (a business referee) and those that make a character reference (a personal referee).

It is usually on the application form itself that the requirements of a referee are specified. The details obtained from any referee must remain strictly confidential and will be most helpful to an organization if the information requested is asked for in a clear and specific way.

Usually, references are made after a job offer, which implies that the job offer is conditional on obtaining satisfactory references.

(7) Other issues

These include:

- *Details should be kept of the whole recruitment process in case of need of reference later on.*
- *As we have seen strict confidentiality throughout is mandatory.*
- *Any unsuccessful candidates should be notified, in writing, as soon as possible.*
- *Job offer letters should be sent out as soon as practically possible.*
- *Any job offer letter must be accurate in terms of detail, and let the successful*

candidate know how long he or she has to accept or decline the offer. Often the preferred start date is also included.

10.6
The Induction Process

An induction process takes place when a new team member goes through a period of training, development and familiarization for a new job. Effectively then the team leader or manager is able to assess the new colleague's suitability for that job. An induction training process is used for all new members of staff, and also part-time staff, contract staff and possibly for those who are returning to work after a period of absence (e.g., maternity leave).

The main aims of the induction process are as follows:

- *To provide the suitable training and support for all the members of staff.*
- *To begin to identify any future training requirements.*
- *To enable the new team member to become as effective as possible, as soon as possible.*
- *To keep full records of the new team member in the early months, probably six months, in order for an effective review of job performance to take place at the end of the probationary period.*

There are some very important stages in the induction training process, and these include:

- *On the first morning – one key responsibility of the team leader is to greet the new colleague when he or she arrives at the business unit, and make sure that he or she is introduced to other colleagues. Usually, the new team member is given 'a tour' of the business unit, either in full or in part, on their first day. This provides an ideal opportunity for the new team member to become familiar with the new surroundings and with the new colleagues. Understandably, the new entrant may be feeling a little apprehensive on the first day, and a sensitive approach needs to be taken so that he or she does not feel either overawed, or 'on show' to the rest of the team. Probably also on the first day, a fairly formal meeting takes place between the new entrant, the team leader and perhaps a 'buddy' who would be asked to take day-to-day responsibility for the new staff member in the early days in work.*
- *During the first fortnight in the early days in work, the new entrant will need some fairly close support from the team leader or manager. It needs to be ensured that he or she has the support necessary to be able to complete all early roles and responsibilities. Regular progress reviews need to be held, probably weekly to*

see how the new entrant is getting on. Additional support could be provided as appropriate. If the new entrant has had a 'buddy' allocated, then the team leader needs to overview this relationship to make sure that it is working in the way intended.

Also, in the early days at work, a new entrant needs to be made aware of the terms and conditions of the new job. Such information should include:

- *Hours of work.*
- *Salary.*
- *Periods of sickness.*
- *Any probationary period.*
- *The appraisal system.*
- *Their key responsibilities (as covered in the job description).*
- *Holidays.*
- *Any bonus or incentive schemes.*
- *Career break details.*

The induction process is a very important stage for the business and the new entrant to the organization. Getting the selection and recruitment policies and approaches correct is merely the start. Once the new recruit has begun work, he or she needs to feel part of the team, part of the organization as soon as possible. Once an organization has recruited somebody it obviously wants that person to stay to the mutual benefit of both the organization and the individual. In any case as we have seen, selection, recruitment and induction policies are very expensive.

Unit 11

Legislation Affecting Team Members

Health and Safety

In every workplace there are inevitably accidents or other health related incidents and, in today's world there are legal systems and procedures which need to be adopted to keep these types of incidents to a minimum.

Factually, approximately ten people are killed at work every week in the UK, every year hundreds of thousands of employees are injured or become ill as a result of accidents. In addition there are many other work related illnesses which may result from, for example, physical/mental stress, working in unhealthy conditions, infections and handling hazardous substances.

The cost to an employee or business of accidents and health problems can be measured in the following terms:

- *Employees off work as a result.*
- *Disrupting the work of other employees.*
- *Recruitment/training costs.*
- *Possible damage to equipment.*
- *Cost of employee absence/welfare benefits.*
- *Possible claims for compensation.*

An employee may also lose out because whilst off work their income may reduce, they may not be able to return to work for a long period of time (sometimes not at all) and there may be additional medical costs.

Overall, it is likely that accidents in the workplace may be caused by:

- *Inadequate supervision.*
- *Poor training.*
- *Lack of clear instructions.*
- *Inadequate procedures.*

It is also immediately clear that policies and procedures are needed to ensure the health and safety of employees whilst at work. The specific reasons why these policies and procedures are needed are:

- *Senior management have this responsibility by law.*
- *Their nominees have the responsibility, again by law, to make sure that the procedures and rules are honoured.*

Legally, every individual in the organization has a responsibility to follow these (legal) rules.

Health problems

In a busy working environment, like a contact centre, the types of health problems that may occur include:

- *Tenosynovitis – essentially a tendon injury which needs to be treated immediately.*
- *Muscle strain – this could happen in the muscles of the neck and shoulders.*
- *Repetitive strain injury – usually as a result of incorrect posture, too heavy workload, repeated movements, having to hold the arms/head, in particular, in a stiff unnatural position, inadequate rest periods.*
- *Visual problems – often caused by having to focus at the same distance for long periods of time (for example, at a VDU) or having to focus at an uncomfortable distance.*
- *Radiation and VDUs – currently the Health and Safety Executive's advice is that there is no particular evidence to show that the users of VDUs need to take special precautions to protect against radiation emissions. Nevertheless, organizations need to make sure that their employees have regular breaks from their work, are encouraged to adjust screen brightness controls to a comfortable level, are encouraged to adjust the position of the screen to a comfortable distance, and ensure that the light from the lamps or windows does not reflect onto the VDU screen itself.*

The law on health and safety

The Health and Safety at Work Act 1974 (HASAWA) is the most important piece of legislation and the two most significant courses are as follows:

- *Section 2 (1) – this section explains that it is the duty of every employer to ensure, as far as possible, the health and safety at work of all of their employees.*
- *Section 2 – this section confirms it is the duty of every employee, whilst in the work place, to take reasonable care for the health and safety of himself and all other employees who may be affected by his actions in the workplace.*

The law imposes a duty on employers to provide any necessary information and training for employees to establish safe practices. This type of information will include:

- *How to work safely in his job.*
- *What to do if something goes wrong.*
- *Where to find safety equipment and how to use it.*
- *What steps he or she needed to take to safeguard the safety of others.*
- *Full awareness and understanding of any special circumstances.*

Employer's statement and safety policy

Legally all organizations need to have:

- *A general health and safety policy statement – this outlines the organization's commitment to health and safety, and its obligations towards its employees. This statement also needs to be clear, in general terms, what the duties of employees are.*
- *Statement of organization – this statement is more specific, outlining who is responsible for particular aspects of health and safety and how the organization is structured.*
- *Statement of arrangements – this is an even more specific statement outlining what actually needs to happen whilst dealing with health and safety issues.*

The employee' duties

These have already been briefly mentioned above but can be further outlined as follows:

- *Each employee must take reasonable care to avoid injury to themselves or to others as a result of their work activities.*

- *Each employee should co-operate with the employers and others in meeting the requirements of the law.*
- *Each employee is legally bound not to interfere or misuse anything which has been provided by the employer to protect their health, safety and welfare.*

The health and safety representative

In many organizations an individual is appointed, usually be a recognised trade union, to represent employees on health and safety issues at work. Obviously, this individual needs to be familiar with the hazards of the workplace and understand fully the particular work being done, so a degree of experience is required (typically two or three years' work experience).

The main responsibilities of this individual will be:

- *Make sure they are fully informed on health and safety related issues.*
- *Encourage co-operation between employer and employees to ensure that measures are introduced and promoted to ensure the health and safety of employees. Systems and checks also need to be agreed and implemented to ensure that these various measures can be checked and monitored.*
- *To bring to the attention of the employer any unsafe or unhealthy conditions or working practices, or unsatisfactory welfare arrangements.*

These representatives will also spend time talking to employees about particular health and safety problems, they will also carry out regular inspections of the workplace to see if there are any real potential hazards which have not been identified or addressed. These representatives will also regularly report to employers about any issues or problems relating to health and safety in the workplace.

We must also remember that in some circumstances an employer is legally obliged to establish a safety committee. Typically, a safety committee would be composed of:

- *A full-time safety officer.*
- *Safety representatives.*
- *Company doctor.*
- *A senior executive of the organization.*

The main functions of this committee would:

- *regularly review the organizations health and safety rules and procedures;*
- *consider and analyze statistics and trends of accidents and health problems;*
- *consider and discuss any reports/information received from health and safety inspectors; and*
- *rigorously scrutinise the effectiveness of the safety content of ongoing employee training.*

Possible conditions in a workplace which may lead to accidents or health problems

Obviously, some issues are fairly generic and could happen in any workplace, and some are more organisation/business unit specific. Some of the likely conditions that could happen in most working environments include:

- *Poor lighting.*
- *Too much/little heating.*
- *Inadequate ventilation.*
- *An untidy workplace.*
- *A dirty workplace.*
- *Wet or slippery floors.*
- *Poor drainage.*
- *Inadequate space for easy movement.*
- *Training tables or other obstacles which employees may trip over.*
- *Protruding corners of furniture.*
- *Dangerous equipment.*
- *Emergency exits blocked.*
- *Poorly designed furniture or work space.*

The responsibilities of a team leader/supervisor

Given the many and various ways in which accidents can happen in the workplace, clearly any team leader has a responsibility for complying with the health and safety rules of the organization. In addition, they will need to be helping team members comply with these rules. Each team leader will need to be setting a good example, give every possible encouragement for their team members to obey the safety rules, they will also need to make sure that safety at work is seen as a priority. Logically therefore every team leader will need to monitor regularly the health and safety performance of their team.

In addition, team leaders will need to:

- *Work with their line manager to agree and maintain standards of safety within their area of responsibility.*
- *Regularly communicate with their team about safety, explaining the rules and answering any questions individual employees may have.*
- *Foster a good team spirit, which is a very good practice in itself, but in addition will enable efforts to be made to improve safety standards.*
- *Ensure individual team members accept their own responsibilities for health and safety, and for that of others.*
- *Ensure each team member reports all incidents, including near misses.*

Security

Security in the workplace may cover many things and will include in many cases the following:

- *Checking the identity of people coming onto the employer's premises.*
- *Searching the bags of individuals entering the premises, where appropriate.*
- *All employees and visitors wearing name badges.*
- *Checking the references of potential new recruits.*
- *Carrying out audits/checks on various systems within the business unit.*
- *Disciplining members of staff for misconduct.*
- *Locking documents away, to prevent any leaks of information to competitors or unauthorised personnel.*
- *Taking necessary actions to avoid theft.*
- *Asking new employees to sign conditions of employment which will include aspects of security.*
- *Fire prevention and fire drills.*
- *Protecting appropriate information and of the Official Secrets Act.*

Clearly this list is not exhaustive, but many of those issues raised will be totally appropriate in a contact centre environment, for example.

Security policy

Many organizations have a formal policy declaration of security and the benefits of this approach are:

- *This policy is a clear statement to all employees about the attitude the organizations has towards security and the seriousness with which it regards breaches of security.*
- *It provides the basis for a co-ordinated overall security policy.*
- *It enables an established starting point to be available, in the event of any dispute about security.*
- *It will give all its employees, in particular managers and supervisors, the confidence to take a positive and specific approach when dealing with potential or real threats to security.*

We also need to be aware that any security policy adopted by an organization will assume the following key points:

- *That it fully recognizes that the vast majority of its employees are honest, and as a result security measures are put in place to protect this majority.*
- *Without doubt security is part of the management/team leader function.*

- *The property of employees must be protected as well as the property of the employer.*
- *In all cases suspected 'offenders' must be seen to be fairly treated.*

In reality some organizations don't protect all of their property, and in some cases it may be impractical to do so. An example would be office employees using the photocopier for private use, or unauthorized telephone calls.

Security of premises

The priority of this particular issue will depend upon the premises occupied by a business or organization. Some of the issues that need to be considered will be:

- *Protecting the building itself.*
- *Adopting a system of requiring everyone who has the right to enter an area to wear an identity badge.*
- *Strict procedures regarding the issue of keys to authorized people.*
- *Having clear signs which advise of danger, for example, around areas with high voltage.*
- *Using a robust system for visitor passes.*
- *Establishing clear procedures in place of how to evacuate the premises in case of need, for example, fire or a bomb scare.*
- *Where appropriate, regular patrolling of ground and premises.*
- *Ensuring contingency arrangements in place should there be a loss of electrical power or air conditioning.*

Security of equipment

Some essential issues to consider here are:

- *Keeping all valuable items under lock and key.*
- *Where appropriate, making individual employees sign for and take responsibility for particular pieces of equipment.*
- *Ensuring all work areas are well lit.*
- *Ensuring only appropriate employees are allowed into 'secure' areas.*
- *Minimising the opportunities for employees to pilfer.*

Security of information

Most major organizations have a major concern about the company security, or data security, particularly relating to illegal access to their computers and potential damage to them.

Possible threats to computer security include:

- *Computer equipment failure.*
- *An environmental disaster – for example, fire, flood.*
- *Electricity failure.*
- *Corruption of data or progams.*
- *An error caused by individual employees, for example, programming errors.*
- *Any illegal practices or sabotage.*

Management can introduce various levels of access control which will mean each employee can only access the information/equipment that they need to. Often passwords are used, which are typically a special combination of letters/numbers issued to authorized people at the relevant level – each individual employee also has their own file number which often has to be used in the access procedures, and therefore clear 'audit trails' are available and kept on record should they be needed.

Security and staff

The main benefits of all employees being aware of the concept of security include:

- *Ultimately, compliance with all aspects of security will protect each individual's own job.*
- *The business/organization security will protect an individual employee's possessions and safety.*
- *In itself the idea of dishonesty will offend the vast majority and should actively be discouraged.*
- *Conversely, any security measures must reinforce the view that the vast majority of employees are basically honest.*

All members of management should therefore take a personal example in leading others in this respect and also:

- *Be consistent and precise in following all of the security rules of the organization.*
- *Be firm but always consistent and fair when dealing with any disciplinary matters.*
- *Co-operate fully with security staff.*
- *Be very clear about the standards of behaviour that are expected from the members of staff for which they have responsibility.*
- *Manage very carefully any secure items under their control.*
- *Ensure any security procedures are rigorously adopted.*
- *'Sell' the idea of security to their team.*
- *Never turn a 'blind eye' to any breaches of security.*

Security and the law

Essentially, the law will define standards of acceptable behaviour and also the way in which security is carried out within an organization must comply with legislation.

Some key examples of Acts of Parliament which have some bearing on security include:

- *Theft Acts 1968 and 1978.*
- *Criminal Law Act 1977.*
- *Restriction of Offensive Weapons Act 1959.*
- *Cheques Act 1957.*
- *Forgery and Counterfeiting Act 1981.*

Therefore this section is concerned primarily with what the legal requirements are, and what typically occurs with any breaches of legislation.

Many organizations use the ACAS code of practice to determine the various levels of offences that have been carried out by individual employees. This code also states that any disciplinary procedures should be:

- *In writing.*
- *Specifically identify to whom they apply.*
- *Be instigated quickly.*
- *Identify clearly which levels of management have the power to take various forms of disciplinary action.*

In addition, all employees have various rights:

- *To be told exactly what they are being accused of and to have the opportunity to state their case/events.*
- *To be represented by a colleague.*
- *To know that they will not be dismissed for a first breach of discipline except in the case of gross misconduct. Gross misconduct will include issues like theft, intoxication, fighting, misuse and abuse of company property.*

Managing Absence

Obviously, in reality, there would be many times when individual employees are unable to get to work. In the vast majority of cases most absences from the workplace are genuine, although as with everything there will be exceptions. A typical exception is when an individual employee's absence will cause concern to their team leader or manager although typically an individual will be away from the office for the following reasons:

- *Sickness.*
- *Family problems.*
- *Work related reasons.*

Quite clearly team leaders and managers need to be fully aware of any individual employees consistent absence from work because the effect is not only upon the individual themselves but also on the day-to-day activities of their colleagues. It is obvious that when any individual is away from work, additional pressure is placed upon their colleagues and there are obviously cost implications. Workplace absence is therefore 'a must' to be managed proactively. Furthermore, if workplace absence is poorly managed, employees across the business unit will see this, and over time, feelings of resentment, de-motivation and discontent will inevitably increase. Others will see the absence being poorly managed and soon start to adopt a 'why bother' approach.

Key principals when managing employee absence from the workplace:

- *Try to ensure that you are aware on the first morning/day that an employee is not going to work and establish the reasons for this. In the majority of cases individual employees will contact work to let them know why they will not be able to attend.*
- *As soon as possible try and establish what the exact problem is, and try and gauge, where possible, how long the employee will be away.*
- *Ensure that if an individual will be away (ill) for more than seven calendar days, that a doctor's certificate is obtained. Prior to this seven-day period, any individual employee is able to 'self certificate' their absence. In periods of longer-term absence, company medical staff often become involved.*
- *Ensure that, as a member of the management team, you keep in regular contact with employees who are away from work unwell. This is usually done by regular, but not too frequent or intrusive, phone calls – each situation needs to be considered on an individual basis.*

Managing the return to work

The best practice to adopt here is, when an individual employee returns to work, their line manager meets with them to discuss how they are feeling, primarily out of a genuine concern for their welfare. Concurrently, this individual, and their colleagues will know that their absence has been noticed and that they have been missed. Clearly, this practice needs to be consistently adopted.

At this 'return to work' interview the manager/team leader will need to:

- *Welcome their colleague back to work.*
- *Confirm the reasons, discretely and sensitively, why the individual was away from work (sometimes a company's personnel department may become involved).*

- *You need to ensure that the individual employee is, in fact, well enough to return to work.*
- *Where appropriate, the manager/team leader may take an individual decision to ease the individual employee back to a full-time role.*
- *It needs to be ensured that this particular interview is not seen either by the employee concerned, or by his colleagues, as an interrogation because there will be clear implications both culturally and around management having a 'lack of trust'.*
- *One key benefit of adopting this fair but firm approach is that it tends to keep abuses of the system to a lower level.*

Absence clearly has impacts on any business unit and as we have said it needs to be carefully and sensitively managed. Team leaders need to be particularly aware of any individuals who appear to take 'regular periods' of time off work due to illness. It may be the case that the system is being abused – although every care needs to be taken that any conclusions drawn on an individual's activities are factually based and not founded on rumours or hunches. Individual abuses of the system do, however, result most often in an informal warning, or in extreme cases a more formal approach is necessary and adopted.

In all cases, it must be that each instance of an employee's absence from the workplace must be treated sensitively and genuinely. There may be cases in which we need to support individual team members, for example, in cases of family illness, poorly children or where compassionate leave may be appropriate. Whatever approach a manager takes, it must be clear, visible and consistent, and based on actual evidence in all cases.

Equal Opportunities

Strictly speaking we are all equal. The reality is probably much different to this. Alternatively, we could consider inequality as being when an individual or group is treated in a less favourable way than another individual or group in a similar type of situation.

It therefore follows that the quality of opportunity in the workplace is important because of:

- *The need to encourage good relationships.*
- *The need to make best use of everybody's abilities.*

The legal situation

Over recent years many laws have been introduced which have clarified the rights of various groups. As a result, concern has been expressed by businesses with regard to the costs that are imposed as a result of these new laws because compliance with such laws are not optional and there are often severe penalties for non-compliance.

Types of individuals protected by law

(a) Women – currently women make up some 45% of the UK's labour force. Research has been consistent to show that women are not always treated well in areas such as opportunities being made available to them for education and training, possibilities for promotion/transfer, and the ways in which they are treated in relation to redundancies.

(b) Racial minorities – this includes someone who may be treated unfavourably because of their race, colour, nationality or ethnic background. Britain is now a multi-cultural nation and whilst, on the whole, relations between racial minorities and the rest of the population are good, research once again shows that inequality of treatment and opportunity in the workplace consistently occurs. This is particularly true in the area of employment, career development, promotion and the specific types of jobs that are available to and taken by individuals from these minorities.

(c) Disabled people – these people are covered by the Disability Discrimination Act 1995. It seems that one of the main reasons why disabled people find it difficult to find jobs or to keep them is primarily due to the attitude of employers rather than with the disability itself. There is still a widely held perception that employers shy away from taking on individuals with a disability because of the fear that they will be 'unreliable' and will need special facilities which have financial implications. The reality, however, can be, and should be, much different to this.

Legal requirements

The law relating to equality in employment is very complex and here we will only be covering the key themes and some of the main laws are as follows:

(1) Sex Discrimination Acts 1975–1986 – this law aims to eradicate discrimination and improvements on grounds relating to gender or marital status.

(2) Race Relations Act 1976 – aims to eradicate discrimination in employment or grounds relating to race or personality.

(3) Equal Pay Act 1970 – this law aims to ensure that both men and women in a particular workplace receive equal pay for the same or similar work.

(4) Employment Protection Act 1978/Employment Act 1980/Social Security Act 1986 – this legislation aims to give pregnant women, or those returning from maternity leave certain rights relating to pay and jobs.

(5) The Disability Discrimination Act 1995 – this law aims to remove discrimination in employment on grounds relating to disability.

You also need to be aware that the law forbids two types of discrimination as follows:

- *Direct discrimination – this is where an individual is treated less favourably than another individual, specifically on the grounds of disability, sex, race, colour, personality, ethnic or national origins.*
- *Indirect discrimination – where employers set conditions for employment which are unnecessary, and have the effect of preventing certain groups from being appointed. In other words, unnecessary conditions that would place individuals of a particular gender or racial group, for example, at a disadvantage.*

In addition to outlawing 'direct and indirect discrimination', the law also forbids:

(a) *Victimization.*
(b) *Pressure to discriminate – where one person or group puts pressure on another to discriminate illegally.*
(c) *Instruction to discriminate – where someone uses their position to instruct illegal discrimination to be carried out.*
(d) *Segregation – which is the isolation of people on racial grounds so that they have to work apart.*

Establishing whether the law has been broken

Quite clearly care needs to be taken here and there needs to be some actions to:

(1) *Show clear evidence around the grounds of a discrimination.*
(2) *Establish what type of discrimination has occurred.*
(3) *Establishing those who are the offenders.*

Achieving the quality of treatment in the workplace

All employees, particularly those at management/team leader levels have a responsibility to ensure that the quality of treatment for all employees is available and evident in the workplace and some issues to consider are:

(1) *Your responsibility to make sure that equal opportunities policies are not just written down and then forgotten about.*
(2) *The main aspects of these policies could be discussed regularly at team meetings.*
(3) *There needs to be a team atmosphere/culture whereby anybody who feels they are being treated unfairly can raise their issue through the appropriate channels.*
(4) *Management and team leaders need to ensure they understand the problems facing certain groups at work.*

(5)   Any possible situation regarding unfair treatment of an employee needs to be assessed objectively and fairly.

(6)   As a manager or team leader you need to, and must, lead by example.

(7)   Your influence as a team leader or manager must be used positively to change unfair situations or scenarios fairly.

(8)   Regular training/guidance should be provided on equal opportunities and the relevant legislation, regular checks should be carried out to make sure that employees are being fairly treated and appropriate records should be kept in case of need.

Individual Rights and Employee Protection

In the area of employment, contracts are crucial as they identify the commitments made by both employer and employee and are often used to clarify any areas of disagreement.

The ACAS (Advisory Conciliation and Arbitration Service) Employment Hand Book lists the following points which should be included in an employee contract:

- Employer's name.
- Place of work/address of employer.
- Employee's name.
- Date on which employment commenced.
- The date on which the employee's period of continuous employment began.
- Clarity regarding employment period should this not be permanent (i.e. for a fixed term).
- Job title.
- The amount of pay and the interval between payments.
- Hours of work.
- Holiday pay/entitlement.
- Sickness and sick pay arrangements.
- Pensions.
- Notice periods.
- A note specifying any disciplinary rules and procedures.
- Details of grievance procedures.
- Details of when and if any travel will be required.

Changing the contract of employment

Changes to a contract of employment would normally be made only if both the employer and employee agree – in some cases an individual employee may wish to take advice from their trade union prior to accepting the change. Similarly, a contract of employment is normally only terminated if both employer and employee agree to do so. It should usually be the case that the employer or employee gives the other party the required notice prior to termination. In extreme circumstances, like for example 'gross misconduct', an individual could be dismissed without notice.

All employees are entitled to at least one month's notice after one month's service, two months' notice after two year's service and an extra one week's notice for every year of employment up to a maximum of 12 weeks for 12 years' service. These periods of notice can be longer if this has been specified in the contract of employment. Again, in some circumstances employees may agree to accept pay instead of working out notice.

The role of the trade unions

Most trade unions are organized at three levels:

- *Branch/business unit level – this is where local members of the trade union can meet and have an opportunity to express their views. These local parts of the union structure usually have a key influence in the decision-making process.*
- *Intermediate level – these groups are likely to be based around particular districts, divisions, regions or areas and their roles tends to be primarily administrative. Also at this intermediate level disputes within or between branches/business units are often resolved. At this 'higher level', trade union policy processes are often instigated or carried out.*
- *Delegate conference – these are usually annual activities where delegates from branches come together in order to finally decide and approve union policies and to elect a national executive committee. This committee is then responsible for administering and controlling the trade union in between conferences and for carrying out the various policies that have been agreed.*

The shop steward/union representative

At local level the union representative with whom individual employers are most likely to liaise is the shop steward – the shop steward should be somebody who is 'acceptable' to both management and union as a representative of trade union members at the local workplace/business unit. Obviously, both local management and the shop steward can clearly influence relationships in the workplace positively or otherwise. The three main aspects of the shop steward's role are as follows:

- *Exactly those of any other full-time employee, because the role of the shop steward is not a full-time activity.*

- To represent any individual in discussions with management about grievances and so on.
- To represent the local business unit in collective negotiations.

It is therefore crucial that local management and shop stewards are able to work together.

Collective bargaining

In many parts of industry trade unions represent their members through a process called collective bargaining. This is where employers and employee representatives agree to negotiate issues whether just pay, conditions of service on a group (organization-wide) basis for the employees in a particular company or industry. Currently, around 40% of the employees in the UK have their wages, terms and conditions of employment determined by collective bargaining.

Union recognition and power

Trade union recognition is agreed after a request from the union to the organization itself and an organization may recognise a union because:

- It already recognizes unions in another part of the organization.
- There is a considerable demand from employees and the majority of employees are union members.
- The organization would view the opportunity of working with the union as a way of consulting and negotiating with their staff.

Trade unions which do not represent a significant proportion of the work force may be granted representation rights rather than full recognition – this means the union is allowed to represent individuals in cases of discipline or grievance.

Where a union is recognised, they will gain certain rights including:

- The right to be consulted prior to employees being made redundant.
- The power to appoint a safety representative.
- Time off for its representative for trade union related activities and duties.

Index